Into the Heart of Life

Books by and about Jetsunma Tenzin Palmo

*Reflections on a Mountain Lake: Teachings on
Practical Buddhism*

Three Teachings

*Cave in the Snow:
Tenzin Palmo's Quest for Enlightenment*
by Vicki Mackenzie

INTO THE HEART OF LIFE

Jetsunma Tenzin Palmo

SNOW LION PUBLICATIONS
ITHACA, NEW YORK

Snow Lion Publications
P.O. Box 6483
Ithaca, New York 14851 USA
607-273-8519
www.snowlionpub.com

Copyright © 2011 Tenzin Palmo

The text of "Eight Verses of Mind Training" that
appears in this work was translated by Ruth Sonam
and published in *Eight Verses for Training the Mind*
by Geshe Sonam Rinchen, translated and edited
by Ruth Sonam (Ithaca, NY: Snow Lion Publications, 2001). Reprinted by permission.

Printed in the USA on acid-free
recycled paper.

ISBN 978-1-55939-374-4

*Library of Congress
Cataloging-in-Publication Data*
Tenzin Palmo, Jetsunma, 1943-
Into the Heart of Life / Jetsunma
Tenzin Palmo.
    pages cm
ISBN-13: 978-1-55939-374-4 (alk. paper)
ISBN-10: 1-55939-374-2 (alk. paper)
1. Religious life—Buddhism.
2. Buddhism—Doctrines. I. Title.
BQ4302.T46 2011
294.3'4—dc22
                                2010052671

❧ Contents

DEDICATION

In devotion to Khamtrul Dongyu Nyima and Khamtrul Shedrup Nyima, who are the Heart of my life.

པདཔལ་རྒྱལ་དབང་འབྲུག་པ།

The Gyalwang Drukpa

15th January 2011

Jetsunma Tenzin Palmo is an accomplished spiritual practitioner and teacher who is able to touch the hearts of many through her teaching and her presence. Even though "Into the Heart of Life" is only a very small collection of the many teachings she has given over the years, it contains the basic principles of how to put Buddha Dharma into practical use.

Buddhist philosophy is sometimes complex and difficult to understand, especially difficult to implement in daily life without clear understanding. Jetsunma has made Buddhist philosophy very easy to comprehend and to be put into practice. For example she explains impermanence as being "not just of philosophical interest. It's very personal. Until we accept and deeply understand in our very being that things change from moment to moment, and never stop even for one instant, only then can we let go." In a simple language, Jetsunma makes everyone understand both impermanence and renunciation.

Throughout the different chapters, she uses practical examples and her own experiences to illustrate the practicality of Buddha Dharma and the need to practise the Dharma with genuine understanding. I am truly amazed at her ability to express complicated philosophical theories in simple words. This is an ability many cannot match, including myself.

The book is well-structured for beginners who are genuinely interested in being happy as well as for advanced practitioners who need to be reminded of the path to happiness.

I want to congratulate Jetsunma for being able to share her understanding of Dharma in daily life and I am certain this book will benefit many. This is a book for everyone who needs and wants to know the path to genuine happiness.

THE GYALWANG DRUKPA

❧ Preface

IN THE MID-1990S on my return to India after an extended stay in Italy, I was requested by the high lamas of my monastery in Tashi Jong to start a nunnery. I asked His Holiness the Dalai Lama what he thought, and he rather optimistically suggested giving it two years before returning to retreat. So I decided to undertake the task, and as I write this in 2010 the nunnery is flourishing with over seventy nuns, although the buildings are still not all completed.

Initially it was very difficult to know how to begin raising interest and funds for a nunnery. I am not an incarnate Rinpoche or even a Tibetan. In addition, I have a female body within a patriarchal tradition. Since I could not bestow empowerments or blessings, what might I offer that could be useful? So I began to deliver Dharma talks, sharing the experience of spiritual practice with audiences made up predominantly of lay people with families, jobs, and a regular social life. This is very different from the times when Dharma was mainly delivered to monastic gatherings.

As I travel around the world, my concern has always been, How can the Dharma be of help to people in everyday life? How can the Dharma be used to lighten our lives and give meaning to our existence? Personally I feel that the world has never had more need of the teachings of the Buddha, overcome as we are with greed, aggression, and emphasis on self-fulfillment—our age-old companions the three poisons.

This book comprises some of the talks that I have delivered over the years to audiences in the East and West who are united in the common challenge to make something meaningful of their lives within the society they inhabit. This is not a book about esoteric practices or advanced methods of meditation. The contents of this book deal with ordinary practitioners concerned with translating Dharma instructions into an ongoing life experience.

An important aspect of the Dharma deals with the transformation of our ordinary minds and attitudes in a highly positive way that will bring benefit not only to ourselves but to all those who have contact with us. The basic problem facing us is how to change a mind filled with negative thoughts and emotions—greed, anger, anxiety, envy, and so on—into a peaceful and more friendly mind that is a pleasure for everyone (including ourselves) to live with. This book sets out in a simple manner some pointers to help ordinary practitioners make use of the Dharma to lead more meaningful lives.

Our mind with its incessant stream of thoughts, memories, opinions, hopes, and fears is our constant companion, from which we cannot escape even in dreams. So it makes sense to cultivate a worthy travel companion for our journey.

❧ I

Impermanence

IN THE SUTRAS there is an account of the Buddha walking with his disciples in the jungle. He leaned down and scooped up a handful of leaves and said to the people around him, "Which is more, the leaves in the jungle or the leaves in my hand?"

The disciples said, "The leaves in the jungle are infinite, and the leaves you are holding in your hand are so few."

The Buddha said, "That is analogous to how much I have realized and how much I am telling you. But still, what I am telling you is all that you need to attain your own liberation."

We should understand that from all the vast expanse of knowledge the Buddha attained when his mind completely opened up in his enlightenment experience, he selected those elements which were the most essential, the most important for us to understand in order to become liberated from this realm of birth and death.

At the beginning of his mission, the Buddha emphasized what are called the three marks or the three signs of existence, three characteristics of everything within our experience which we habitually and persistently deny. The first sign of existence is dissatisfaction. Life as we normally lead it in our confused and very disturbed manner is not satisfactory. It is *dukkha*. Dukkha is the opposite of *sukha*, which means ease, pleasure, everything going nicely. It doesn't exactly mean happiness; it is more a sense of things going smoothly. And dukkha is the opposite of that. It is dis-ease. It's when things don't go the way we want them to go. But of course things unfold as they do whether we like it or not. This underlying dissatisfaction is one of the main qualities of our existence as unenlightened beings.

The second sign of existence is impermanence. The third sign of existence is that nothing in itself has self-existence. In other words, we try to solidify everything. We try to solidify external objects, and we especially try to solidify ourselves. Almost automatically we create a seemingly solid inner core which we call "I" and set everything to revolve around: I think this; I feel this; I am this; this is mine; this is who I am. We usually never ask ourselves, "Who is this *I*, this spider in the center of the web?"

Impermanence. We try to make things stay the way they are; we cling to the idea of permanence. We are normally very resistant to the idea of change, especially the change in what we value. Of course, we like things to change when it's something we don't like, but when it's something we do like, then we hold on.

There are various levels of change, of course. There is gross change—the weather is constantly changing; the seas are changing all the time; the land is changing. Over time, everything is completely transformed. There is the more subtle change in our everyday life, where things are always happening. Relationships, homes, and possessions come and then we lose them. Our bodies change. We start off as tiny, helpless, vulnerable beings and then we grow up. We mature; we age; we die.

And there is the still more subtle momentary change. Nothing actually stays the same for two instants at a time. Life is as a river, always flowing. Heraclitus, the Greek philosopher, said that no man ever steps into the same river twice. But in fact the same man can never step into the river twice. Everything is changing. On account of that we suffer.

Life is unsatisfactory because it is always changing. It doesn't have this solid core which we always hope to grasp. We want security, and we believe that our happiness lies in being secure. And so we try to make things permanent. We get houses which seem very permanent and we furnish them. We get ourselves into relationships which we hope will last forever. We have children and hope they may also consolidate this idea of an identity, something which will be constant. We have children, and we love our children, so our children will love us, and this will carry on for a long, long time all through our lives. Our children are our security.

But there is no security in this, because security is very insecure. True security only comes from comfort with insecurity. If we are at ease with the flow of things, if we are at ease with being insecure, then that is the greatest security, because nothing can throw us off balance. As long as we try to solidify, to stop the flow of the water, to dam it up, to keep things just the way they are because it makes us feel safe and protected, we're in trouble. That attitude goes right against the whole flow of life.

Everything changes, moment to moment to moment. Even in physics we learn that objects, which seem so solid and so stable, are actually in a constant state of motion. Objects are not stable; they don't remain fixed and unchanging, although our senses give us the distorted impression that they do so.

We look at each other. Today I see you. And tomorrow, you will look the same to me. But you're not the same. So much has been going on, even on the cellular level, through that time. Cells grow and they die; they are always changing. And we're always changing, too, in the mind, from moment to moment to moment. Although we try to solidify things and keep them just the way they've always been, as that makes us feel very safe, we can't do it. It's like those old castles. We build very thick solid walls and think they're going to last forever, that no onslaught will ever change them. But that's a delusion. Even if we try to hold on to the river that is our life, it will flow away anyway. We can't hold on to the river by grasping at it. The way to catch the river is to hold very lightly.

It's not necessary to suffer. When we suffer, we suffer because our minds are deluded and because we don't see things as they really are. We have fear, the fear of losing, and we have grief when we lose. But it's the nature of things to come into being, to last awhile, and then to go.

Our culture finds this question of losing very difficult. It's very good about getting. Our consumer culture, especially nowadays, is all about getting, getting, getting. We throw away those things which were fashionable yesterday but are no longer fashionable today to get something new. We don't have that attitude, though, toward our own bodies or the bodies of others. We don't think that we too need to be recycled from time to time, but we do. It's ironical that in our society everybody talks very openly about sex, which in other societies is a big taboo. But in our society, the big taboo is death.

I was brought up in a Spiritualist family. My mother was a Spiritualist, and we held séances at our house every week. In my house, death was an everyday subject; it was a topic which we talked about with a great deal of enthusiasm and interest. It wasn't morbid. And on those few occasions in my life when I really thought, "Now I'm about to die," my next reaction has always been, "Let's see what happens." I think that is because as a child death was an open subject. I'm deeply grateful for this, because in our society, talk of death generally makes people feel uncomfortable. So many people are afraid of it for themselves and for others. We don't accept that everything which comes into being lasts awhile and then goes. But that's the cycle. Everything is impermanent. And it's our non-acceptance of this which brings us grief. We live in our relationships, torn between our hopes and our fears because we hold on so tightly, so afraid to lose.

Everything is flowing. And this flow isn't made up only of external things. It includes relationships, too. Some relationships last for a long time, and some don't—that's the way of things. Some people stay here for some time; some people leave very quickly. It's the way of things.

Every year millions and millions of people are born and die. In the West, our lack of acceptance is quite amazing. We deny that anyone we love could ever be lost to us. So often we are unable to say to someone who is dying, "We're so happy to have had you with us. But now, please have a very happy and safe journey onwards." It's this denial which brings us grief.

Impermanence is not just of philosophical interest. It's very personal. Until we accept and deeply understand in our very being that things change from moment to moment, and never stop even for one instant, only then can we let go. And when we really let go inside, the relief is enormous. Ironically this gives release to a whole new dimension of love. People think that if someone is unattached, they are cold. But this isn't true. Anyone who has met very great spiritual masters who are really unattached is immediately struck by their warmth to all beings, not just to the ones they happen to like or are related to. Non-attachment releases something very profound inside us, because it releases that level of fear. We all have so much fear: fear of losing, fear of change, an inability to just accept.

So this question of impermanence is not just academic. We really have to learn how to see it in our everyday lives. In the Buddhist practice of mindfulness, of being present in the moment, one of the things which first strikes one is how things are constantly flowing, constantly appearing and disappearing. It's like a dance. And we have to give each being space to dance their dance. Everything is dancing; even the molecules inside the cells are dancing. But we make our lives so heavy. We have these incredibly heavy burdens we carry with us like rocks in a big rucksack. We think that carrying this big heavy rucksack is our security; we think it grounds us. We don't realize the freedom, the lightness of just dropping it off, letting it go. That doesn't mean giving up relationships; it doesn't mean giving up one's profession, or one's family, or one's home. It has nothing to do with that; it's not an external change. It's an internal change. It's a change from holding on tightly to holding very lightly.

Just recently, I was in Adelaide, Australia, and somebody handed me a cartoon strip which showed how to hold things. The first cartoon was about holding things gently, like a newborn chick; the second cartoon addressed different ways of holding things skillfully, with honor and respect, but not tightly. And then the last cartoon said, "After that, we have to let go. But that's a whole other thing—we'll deal with that later!"

Yes, we have to know how to hold things lightly, and with joy. This enables us to be open to the flow of life. When we solidify, we lose so much. Engaged in a relationship with our partner, our children, and with others in this world, we may solidify them by casting them in certain roles. That's how we see them. And after a while, we no longer experience the real person in the moment. We just see our projection of that person. Even though they are completely unique, and even though they may actually be transforming and changing within, we don't see that any more, because all we see is our pattern. And then people get bored with each other, or at least they get kind of locked into a relationship which has lost its early vitality. As I said, that's because we don't experience the actual moment; we just experience our version of events.

When we look at something, we see it for a moment but then immediately our judgments, our opinions, our comparisons step right in. They become filters between us and the person or object we are looking at, and these filters take us further and further away from what is. We're left with our own impressions and ideas, but the thing in itself is gone. This is especially true when our subject is other people.

We all know that when people are relating an event, it's almost as though each person is telling a different story. We've all had the experience of listening to someone tell of an event that was shared in common, and thought something like, "It didn't happen like that!" "They didn't say that," or, "It wasn't like that at all; you completely missed the point!" In other words, everything becomes incredibly subjective. We don't see the thing in itself; we just see our version. And nowhere is this reflected more clearly than in our resistance to the fact that we are all changing moment to moment. It's as though the carpet is continually being pulled from under our feet, and we can't bear that. "That carpet is going to stay just where I want that carpet to stay. That same carpet, under the same feet." And because that can't ever happen, because we can never, however much we delude ourselves, have things exactly the same, we have this pain.

It's so important to understand that our happiness and peace of mind do not come from seeking security in permanence and stability. Our happiness comes rather from finding security in the ever-changing nature of things. If we feel happy and thus able to be buoyant in the current, nothing can ever upset us. But if we build something so rigid that we don't want it ever to change—a relationship, our job, anything—then when we lose it, we're completely thrown off balance. Normally, people think that the constant change of things is something frightening. But once we really understand that it's actually the very nature of things to flow, to change, then we become completely balanced and open and accepting. It's when we try to dam up the stream that the water becomes very stagnant. We have to let things flow. Then, the water is always fresh and clear.

When I went to India for the first time I found work as a volunteer at the Young Lamas Home School teaching young tulkus, or incarnate lamas. After that, I went to live with my lama, Khamtrul Rinpoche. I was ordained and then I worked with him for six years as a nun and as his secretary. Although I didn't have any money, he always gave me room and of course, food. I was taken care of. Then the community moved to their present site of Tashi Jong. At that time the land was a tea estate; nothing yet had been built on it, and everyone in the community was living in tents. Khamtrul Rinpoche said to me, "During the next year, it would be a good idea if you didn't come to Tashi Jong yet as there's nowhere for you to stay. So you go off and do your own thing for a year and then come back after we've got some buildings." The whole community went to Tashi Jong, and I was left behind, in a hill station called Dalhousie. I remember standing on a hill looking out over the plains on one side and the mountains on the other, and for a moment feeling totally desolate. My lama had gone. The community had gone. I had no family there; I had no friends there. I had no money, and nowhere to stay. I didn't know what to do. I thought, "Oh dear—." And then I thought, "My whole life is given to the Buddha, Dharma, and Sangha. Gampopa said that anyone who practices the Dharma, anybody on a genuine spiritual path, will never starve." So I told myself, "All right. I've handed over my whole life to the Buddha, Dharma, and Sangha, so let them take care of it." And I felt this tremendous sense of reassurance that it was perfectly all right to be insecure.

In that moment, I really got an insight into the fact that real security lies not in clinging to security but in feeling secure within that insecurity.

Just in that moment, there was a tremendous sense that it was okay to just allow things to be. I thought, "Don't worry." This was very personal. And I don't mean to suggest that you all have to do it like this. Many of you have families and friends, so it may be different for you. But there was a very strong sense that if from my side I didn't worry, if from my side I wasn't concerned about not having anywhere to live and not having any money, and if I just carried on devoting my life to the Buddha, Dharma, and Sangha, things would work out. And of course things did work out, and things have continued to work out through these past thirty years.

We have very little faith in the universe. Faith here doesn't mean that we just sit back and don't do anything, but rather that we understand the scale of things happening. We don't actually have to do everything ourselves. If we can plug into this—I don't know what to call it, a kind of universal energy—of itself things will be taken care of. But if we try to do everything by ourselves, then this universal energy sort of backs off and says, "Okay, you get on with it."

Do you understand?

If we are genuinely directing ourselves from the heart to something truly good and we really have faith in that, then what we need comes. It's not that we're going to become Bill Gates. We'll probably always remain poor, but it doesn't matter, because life isn't about getting lots of wealth and possessions, as you all know. But we have to have faith that these things will come to us as we need them if from our side we are doing what we need to do in this world. And this has to do with the question of impermanence, because it means that as things in life change, we are able to change with them.

We have all experienced the ability to be flexible, to be open and to let go of things in order to change direction if necessary. It's the rigidity which causes trouble. And this brings us to the next important question of our precious human existence. More and more, our commodity-oriented society is trying to convince us that we're here in order to have a good time, and to get more and more of whatever it is that the big businesses are churning out. It doesn't matter how junky it is: if it's this year's fashion, we've got to want it. But we don't just have to want it, we've got to work hard and buy it. We think that will give us happiness; we think that is what happiness means.

Many of us who have inquired into the nature of impermanence have rejected this. Congratulations. Because most of the world hasn't. Certainly most of the third world is just arriving at this deluded belief that the more material goods one has, the happier one will be. Many people, regardless of their place in the world, believe that the meaning of their life is to be successful and that success means to be comfortable and wealthy. It means to have more or less all the things we want, like nice relationships, with everything going just the way we want: good health, happiness, and enough money to spend on all the things we want. And if we can manage to get that, then it's a good happy life. But the fact is that we have human potential, which has to do with our intelligence and our ability to have endless compassion for others. Our unfolding human potential allows us to really direct our lives to something meaningful, something more profound, something inner. If we just direct all our energies and activities to being happy, pleasant, and comfortable, we're no different from the animals.

In the *Life of Milarepa*, the story of Tibet's great yogi of the eleventh century, we read that once, when he was sitting in his cave, a very frightened deer came running in. Milarepa sings to comfort the deer, and the deer sits down beside him. A while later, a hunting dog runs into the cave, avidly looking for the deer. Milarepa sings to the dog, too, and the dog calms down and sits on his other side. Then a huntsman comes storming in—his name is Gonpo Dorje. My lama Khamtrul Rinpoche is said to be an incarnation of Gonpo Dorje. The huntsman comes in and roars with anger to see the deer and the dog sitting so peacefully side by side. He tries to shoot at Milarepa to kill him. But of course Milarepa is impervious to arrows. After a while, the huntsman calms down a bit and Milarepa sings to him as well. Milarepa declares, "It is considered that the human life is precious, but I don't see anything precious about you!" Later, Gonpo Dorje becomes one of his greatest disciples.

Isn't that true of so many people we know? We have this precious human life, and what are we doing with it? Where is it precious? Our human life is only precious if we use it in a way which is meaningful. Otherwise, it's not a precious life. It is not precious merely because we're human. It's only precious and rare if we make use of it in a meaningful way.

We are here. Honestly, I can't say I know why we are here. Who knows why? But at least, while we *are* here, let's use what we have as a learning process, because the one thing about a human birth is that we have choice.

According to Buddhist cosmology, there are twenty-six heavenly realms and eighteen hells of various types. The beings down in the hell realms are so tormented by their sufferings they can think only about themselves. The beings in the heavenly realms are so seduced by pleasure that they have no incentive to improve themselves. And the animals don't have the intelligence to be able to have self-awareness in the same way as human beings. But human beings have this mixture of pain and pleasure. And because of this, we can learn. We have choice. With everything that happens to us, we have a choice as to how we'll respond; whether we respond skillfully or unskillfully is up to us. Moment to moment we are creating our lives for ourselves. Sometimes people get so caught in ruts that they feel they can't escape, can't get out. But of course this is not actually true—we can.

I write to a number of prisoners in America. They are as entrapped as anyone can be. They are in situations where they're often surrounded by very unsympathetic fellow prisoners and guards. One prisoner in Texas, though, started a small Dharma group of like-minded prisoners. They wanted to sit and meditate and to have a little Dharma discourse. It took them six months of pleading before the guards gave them permission to sit on the floor. Imagine: they had a hard time getting permission even to meet, even to just sit on the floor. "No, you can't sit on the floor. Why do you want to sit on the floor? That is weird." But even within seemingly inflexible situations, situations from which they can't physically escape, the prisoners are inwardly transformed. They are sincerely using these very adverse circumstances to grow, to deepen their understanding, to expand their compassion, and to look into their past and see where they went wrong. They are learning how not make those same mistakes again in the future. This is what being human is about. This is why our human life is so precious. We can do that. And it's why we should not waste this opportunity by just being mindless. This is a time when we can expand by leaps and bounds, even when things are very adverse—sometimes, *especially* when things are adverse.

When everything is going well, we can be lulled into thinking that we're much nicer and more advanced than we actually are. When everyone is pleasant to us, when circumstances are all going well, when all our relationships are congenial, then it's very easy to think, "I'm basically a nice person and everything's all right and I'm full of loving-kindness and compassion." But it's when things don't go right, when people don't do what we want, when things don't work out the way we've planned—that's when we learn. That's when we really see where we're at, how far our compassion extends and how much our patience really exists or doesn't exist. When people are mean to us or rude to us or cheat us or leave us, we have a chance to see this.

We need these things. It's not that we have to go out and look for painful experiences or obnoxious people—they will come to us! And when they do come, we should have a mind which is able to absorb, understand, accept, and use that, not a mind which runs away or tries to avoid, or just generates more negativities. This is our opportunity.

Shantideva, a seventh-century Buddhist philosopher in India, said in the *Bodhicharyavatara (The Way of the Bodhisattva)* that this earth is full of stones and thorns. It is very painful to walk on. So what are we to do? Do we carpet the whole world? That would be very difficult, as there is a lot of ground out there. But we don't need to carpet the whole world; we just have to put leather on the soles of our feet—shoes—and we can walk anywhere. Likewise, we can't rid the world of all adverse circumstances and difficulties. There are billions of other people in the world, and there is only one of us. But we don't need to change everybody. All we have to do is transform our own mind. When our mind is transformed, everything is transformed.

One way of transforming our minds, apart from developing such qualities as patience, understanding, and tolerance, is to really see that this life we have here is very precious. It is very precious because it is our workroom: here we will make advancements if we want to, in whatever station of life we find ourselves.

We can use every moment of this life. Sometimes people have the idea that practice means going to Dharma centers or sitting in meditation or performing rituals and this sort of thing. They think that all this is practice while the rest of the day is a waste of time. People think there is this big split, and they often despair, feeling that their families and their children are obstacles that keep them away from the spiritual life. But the fact is, especially in this present day, we have to accept the situation we are in and use that as our spiritual path. Of course, meditation is very important, but it's not the only means needed in order to become an enlightened being. We need to develop other qualities also. We need to develop a really open heart, a generous heart, a heart which is accepting and patient. We have to have very clear ethical conduct, living in this world so that we never harm others in any way. Neither do we harm ourselves. We must live a very harmless life, not just thinking of ourselves but caring for others, so that with each being we meet, our first feeling is, "May you be well and happy." It doesn't matter whether it's someone we know or don't know, or even someone we dislike. May you be well and happy. We can all generate that sense of good will. If we generate that, then slowly, slowly, everything we do in our life is transformed into practice.

We have this lifetime—this is what we have. How are we going to use it? Are we going to use it skillfully, or are we just going to waste it? It's up to us. We can't blame our families, our friends, our parents, our upbringing, our social status, or the government. It's up to us. Happiness and unhappiness depend on the individual. What we do with the circumstances we find ourselves in is up to us. For example, even if we have a very life-threatening disease, we have a choice: either we go under with complete despair, frustration, and anger, or we say, "Well, what a wonderful opportunity this is giving me to realize that we are all finite, that we are all going to die. So what is important and what is not important in life? This disease gives me the opportunity to clear up my relationships, tie up loose ends, and also really focus on that which is important to me." Instead of feeling angry at one's disease, one can feel almost grateful. One can use it. One can use anything.

Each one of us is responsible for our own life, and for helping and giving love and understanding to those who are closest around us. Our family, our children, our partners, our parents—they are our practice. They are not an obstacle to our practice. They are the ones who need our loving-kindness, our compassion, our patience, our joyous effort. Our wisdom. It's not so difficult to sit and meditate on loving-kindness and compassion for all those sentient beings out there somewhere on the horizon. But the sentient beings for whom we really have to generate loving-kindness and compassion are the ones who are right in front of us, especially those for whom we are most karmically responsible. They are our objects of practice.

Our everyday life is our spiritual life. If we have the awareness to be able to use our everyday life as practice, then our lives have meaning. Otherwise, the days go by—impermanence, as we know—moment to moment to moment, day after day, year after year, and suddenly, there we are, faced with death, and what have we done? We don't know when we are going to die. Every breath we take could be our last breath: we don't know. When we wake up in the morning, we should say, "How amazing that I didn't die during the night," and when we go to sleep at night, we should say, "How amazing that I lasted this whole day and I haven't died yet." Who knows when we'll die?

We honestly don't know. All these people killed in accidents on the road—did they think they were going to die? Death comes without respect for age or success or beauty or health. When we go, we go. So we have to live each day as if it were our last. If we really thought, "Tomorrow, I'm going to die," what would we do with today? Surely we would really start to re-evaluate our whole situation.

Once when I was in my cave, there was a raging blizzard and I was snowed in. The blizzard blew seven days and seven nights non-stop and the cave was completely covered. When I opened the window, there was just a sheet of ice; when I opened the door, there was a sheet of ice. I thought, "This is it," because the cave was very small and I would surely run out of oxygen and die. So I got myself all ready. I got out these little pills you're supposed to take at the time of death (although I have to say, those little pills are rock hard!), and I went through my life. I regretted the things I had done wrong, and I rejoiced in the things I had done right. It was very salutary because I really believed that I only had a day or two left at the most. It really put things into perspective—what was important and what was not important; what was important for me to think and what was totally irrelevant for me to think. Normally our minds are filled with non-stop chatter, the running commentary of totally useless soap-opera dialogue that we present to ourselves. But when we believe we've only got a limited amount of time to keep thinking, we become very discriminating in our thoughts, and much more conscious of how we're using our time and of what we're doing with our mind.

If we live thinking that each day is our last, it helps us appreciate each moment. This is not being fatalistic or gloomy. If this was our last day on earth, we would be careful of our time. We wouldn't create more problems; we would try to solve the problems we already have. We'd be nice to people. If we're not going to see them again, why not be nice to them? Wouldn't we be kind to our family, our children, our partners, and the people that we're leaving, if we thought we were never going to see them again? Because, who knows? We might not. One day, we won't.

Why not be ready?

✒ QUESTIONS

Q: You mentioned just now being able to discriminate various thoughts as they come up in the process of meditation. What actually happened in your mind for you to develop the ability to see that?

JTP: Well, we all have that ability. The thing is that as one is sitting and looking at the mind itself, thoughts come, feelings come, emotions come. At first, they are the surface thoughts and the surface emotions, but later, as the mind turns deeply into buried emotions or thoughts, it's very clear that every thought and emotion that we experience has a tonal quality to it which is either pleasant or unpleasant and we can see very clearly what thoughts are wholesome and what thoughts are unwholesome.

The Buddha said that there are four right efforts: the effort to rid oneself of negative thoughts when they arise; the effort to prevent future negative thoughts from arising; the effort to cultivate good thoughts which we already have; and the effort to increase their occurrence. Now, we can only do that if we have a fairly good idea of the contents of our mind. We have to be aware. We can see as thoughts and emotions come up that some of them are destructive—they're negative, they're of no use to us, and they don't help us in any way. When we see in the moment the feeling of anger or strong attachment arising—if we really see it—when we absolutely know it and recognize it, then in that moment before we start commenting on it, it will of itself transform.

Q: That's interesting. Did that take a long time in your cave?

JTP: Well, actually, no. The first time it happened was before I went into the cave. But it was during a time when I was suffering very much from attachment. Suddenly, in the moment, I saw the whole thing. It was a moment of clarity and understanding. In that moment, the whole thing fell apart and never came again.

Q: All the meditation in your cave from then on was developing around that one single insight?

JTP: In a way, it showed me that it was possible. After that, of course, one has other moments of insight, but it never went quite as deep and completely final as that one. But at that moment, it was very clear. It's as if we have a rope which is made up of many strands, then several strands snap and we feel the rope give—it's still actually connected, but we feel it give. It was just like that. Something inside dropped away and never re-formed again. It was an absolute moment of major clarity. In one way, that's what we're also trying to do with really seeing, because in the moment of seeing is the moment of liberation. But normally we don't see because our minds are cluttered. We have too many commentaries, biases, thoughts, feelings, ideas, and conceptions which keep covering the actual experience.

Meditation gives space in the mind; it gives us the space to experience. Normally, our lives are so cluttered that we don't even have breathing space. But meditation gives us the breathing space so that things can arise, so that understanding and experiences can come up. Normally, we're so busy that they can't surface, because there is no room. So the majority of meditation is just sitting and sitting. Nothing is happening, but we just sit with the non-happening and give space. Whether anything happens or doesn't happen, it doesn't matter—at least we're present in the moment with what is happening, even if it isn't much.

Especially nowadays, the one thing we don't have in our everyday lives is space, silence. We don't hear ourselves anymore because we are so completely inundated with external and internal noise. Meditation is about coming back to our silent inner spaciousness.

Q: I'd like to ask about ethical misconduct. I'm wondering if there are some practices you can do if you haven't quite got that completely developed?
JTP: Of course, otherwise we'll never get down to doing practices! Because if we're leading relatively unethical lives—getting drunk every day, or having wild affairs, or being caught up in painful, tricky relationships, or losing our temper frequently—in any way being quite immoral, it would be difficult to sit and make the mind quiet and tranquil. So it makes sense to get our ethical life together as much as we can. The point is, once we begin to actually cultivate the mind, that helps us to lead a more ethical life. The two go hand in hand.

I mentioned ethics because it's so important, and because nowadays many modern Buddhists tend to put it to one side, saying, "Oh, that's not important. Meditation is the only thing." But we can't really meditate if we're leading a life which is out of control. The Buddhist precepts are not commandments—"Thou shalt not." The actual wording says, "I undertake to observe the rule of training." And that's what precepts are: rules of training. The five precepts are based on the naturally spontaneous conduct of an enlightened being. An enlightened being wouldn't dream of intentionally killing or stealing or doing any of these other harmful things. What we're trying to do is to bring our own life into balance and to reflect on the way in which someone with wisdom would naturally act. To live in this world as harmoniously as possible so that anything—any beings, even insects—can come into our presence and know that they're safe with us. All beings may know they can trust us. We won't try to take anything from them, or harm them in any way, or cheat them, or abuse them for our own gratification. They're safe with us. That's a very beautiful way in which to live. And with a peaceful mind which is not guilt-ridden, one can sit down to practice.

When we make our slips—as we all do, because we are human beings and imperfect—then we regret it, and we try to do better the next time and not keep repeating the same mistakes. We understand that this is not skillful behavior. It doesn't lead to happiness, and it doesn't lead us in the direction we want to follow. So then we try to get ourselves back on track again. We try to learn from that experience and go on.

Of course there's no celestial Buddha up there with a thunderbolt glaring at us if we go off track a bit. It's not like that. But there are karmic results of our actions, and it makes sense to lead a life which really does benefit ourselves and others. These precepts are not about issues that were only relevant 2500 years ago in India; they are totally applicable today. They have nothing to do with social times or cultural biases. These precepts simply express how an enlightened being would act.

✍ 2

Karma, or Cause and Effect

L ET US EXPLORE the nature of karma, because I think karma is quite
misunderstood in the West. There are various understandings in
different religious traditions of the meaning of *karma*, but here we'll examine
the Buddhist understanding of that term. Actually, the word *karma* in Sanskrit means "action." It also means "work."

All actions we undertake not only with our body but with our speech and
with our mind are expressions of karma. It's the action part that counts, not
the result.

The Buddha himself said that by *karma* he meant intention, *chetana*. Karma
is intention. This means that every intentional action of body, speech, or
mind plants seeds in our mind stream. Sooner or later, in that lifetime or
in future lifetimes, those seeds will sprout and ripen. That ripening is called
vipaka, which means a result of the karma. And that is what we experience.
We have to understand that karma isn't some kind of overpowering or all-
pervading fate. The little seeds planted in the past are eventually going to
sprout up. How and when they sprout is undetermined.

When the Lord Buddha Siddhartha Gautama attained enlightenment it
wasn't just a sudden zap. It was a very gradual opening of the mind. In the
first watch of the night as he sat under the Bodhi Tree in Bihar, he went back
through all his previous births. He went through aeons and aeons of time,
through devolutions and evolutions of the universe, back through billions
of years, knowing: *At that time, I was like this. At that time, I lived like this and
then I died, and I was reborn like that.* Time has no meaning on an absolute
level, and so in a very short time he was able to experience all this. Then,
in the second watch of the night—a watch is a three-hour period—his mind
opened still further to encompass all beings: their coming into existence,

their duration, their passing away and coming again into a new being. And in the third watch of the night, just before dawn, he realized the interconnection and the relativity of all things: interdependent origination. That is when he became a Buddha.

Nowadays in our very humanistic, scholastic mode we say, "Oh well, the Buddha talked about karma because it was the fashion of the day. You know, everybody in those days believed in karma, or many people did, so he just took it on board as part of his doctrine." But it wasn't like that. It was part of his enlightenment to actually experience how beings come and how beings go, and how they are interrelated and interconnected—how karma works. Later on, his main attendant and cousin, Ananda, said to him, "Well, karma is kind of complicated, but I think I've got it now." The Buddha replied, "Don't even say that. The understanding of karma is the province only of the mind of a fully enlightened one."

Only a Buddha can really understand karma, because only a Buddha can see the total pattern, the whole tapestry. We just see a tiny part, and on the wrong side usually—the side with all the knots and the loose ends. And then we try to understand the total pattern from that tiny square, but how is that possible? We need to look at the other side at a distance in order to see how all those red and green and blue threads form a pattern. I don't mean that our life patterns are already woven. We are continually weaving. That's the whole point.

The Buddha said that karma is intention. This means that the seeds we sow are influenced not by the actual overt action, but by the motivation behind that action. Whenever we do anything, we can always justify it to ourselves. We always have high and moral reasons for doing whatever we do, and we can usually think of excuses for much of our conduct. But what is the real, underlying reason for what we do and say and think? Because it is that, the genuine reason, not the reason by which we justify ourselves, which is going to color and influence the kinds of seeds that are being sown. That's one reason why mindfulness is so emphasized in Buddhist practice: we have to become aware not only of the superficial actions, thoughts, and ideas, but of what is really going on underneath. In order to make things very simple, Buddhist psychology divides these motivations into what are called the six roots; three negative roots and three positive roots are seen as underlying incentives for all our actions. Although it's a great simplification, it's amazing how such classification does actually clarify what we do and say and think.

The three negative roots are our old friends the three poisons. That means basic delusion or confusion, greed or desire, and anger or hatred. Any action we perform with an underlying motivation of delusion, greed, or ill will is negative, and it will result eventually in negative effects. Actions we perform with the opposite of that are traditionally known as non-delusion, non-greed, and non-ill will. That means we engage in actions with understanding, or clarity of mind; detachment, or generosity (the opposite of greed is generosity, which means wanting to share and to give, rather than to keep it all for oneself); and loving-kindness and compassion. These three wholesome roots will eventually bring a very good harvest. Therefore, it is necessary for us to understand what we are doing and why we are really doing it, and to allow as much clarity into the situation as possible.

From a Buddhist point of view, we have all lived countless lifetimes in so many different forms—as male and female, as human beings and as animals, as spirits, and as all sorts of things. There is almost nothing we haven't done at some time. This is one reason why we're so connected with all beings—we've shared their experiences at some time, even though we've now forgotten them. Sometimes we are high, sometimes we are low; sometimes we are poor, sometimes we are rich; sometimes we are very clever, sometimes we are stupid. We've done it all. Sometimes we are nice people, and sometimes we're absolutely awful. Who are we to condemn when we have probably experienced everything at some time or another?

And because we have planted so many diverse seeds, even if in this lifetime we've been really good people, it may be that we have to experience the results of a crop which we sowed at some previous time, one which was very negative. So, despite the fact that we're very good people—we've always been kind and generous—we may yet have a life which is difficult and full of problems, maybe a life with ill-health, or with people cheating us, or whatever. We may feel that this is very unfair: "I'm such a nice person, how can this happen to me?" The reason is that we were not always nice people. Sometimes, we've been horrible people. Therefore we have to experience the fruition of those past actions. And we should be grateful, because if we respond with a positive mind now, we transform them from hardship into a teaching on the path, as a way of learning patience and cultivating compassion for the sufferings of others, too. Then we not only plant good seeds for the future, but we exhaust the bad seeds of the past.

I had a friend who had breast cancer. On the whole, I'm sure she had been a really nice person in her lifetime. She led a good and wholesome life. So she could well have thought, "Why is this happening to me? I'm so young, and yet look at this—what a very terrible thing to happen to me." But once, when she was resting, she had a waking dream in which suddenly she found herself as a man: she was now a soldier in armor standing over another soldier, who was lying on the ground. He had a red cross on his breastplate, as if it was during the time of the Crusades. Holding a spear to his chest, she was looking down at him. He was pleading for his life, and she knew at that moment she had a choice. She could let him go or she could kill him. She looked into his eyes and his eyes looked into hers, and he was imploring. She thrust the spear right through him. And as she did that, she felt such an incredible pain at her chest, and then she awoke into present-day consciousness.

Whether or not that was just something which her mind brewed up, who knows? But it could also be an explanation for why so many centuries later, she was now having this terrible disease. In this lifetime she was a good person. But we plant seeds, and they have to come up once the right conditions appear. We have to accept that.

And that brings us to the next part of this whole question. Now we are here, and we have this lifetime. We don't come into this world as empty blank sheets, no matter what the psychiatrists like to tell us. I'm sure those of you who have had children know very well that each child is very different right from the start. We look into the eyes of a small baby, and it's a person! We bring with us the patterning and conditioning of many, many lives.

Therefore in this lifetime there will be certain things which happen to us; certain events which are likely to occur. But there are infinite crossroads; it's not all laid out. We are going along, and the road branches. If we take this path then we will go on and we will meet more turnoffs. Or if we take that path, we will meet with other turnoffs, and so on. It's like that. It's not as though one way has already been set out for us, one way predestined for us. Some people have the kind of lives which look like that. For instance, my own life has always seemed a bit predestined, presumably because of very strong imprints and aspirations from the past. When I try to make a detour, barriers come up, and I have to keep going the way I am supposed go. But nonetheless, we do have choice. This is the point of a human birth—we have choice. Even people who have clairvoyance say, This is only what is likely to happen. It doesn't have to happen; other circumstances can come up and we can change it. For example, at one time the Buddha was walking outside the city walls, and he saw a ragged corpse. It was the body of a drunken wastrel who had just died. The Buddha said that this man, the son of a rich merchant, had originally been very wealthy. He had met with the Buddha, and was attracted to the Dharma, and had even thought of becoming a monk. But his wife dissuaded him and so he didn't ordain. Eventually he began to gamble and drink and waste all his money. He ended up as a beggar. The Buddha said that if he had become a monk at that time, he would have become an Arhat. He would have become completely liberated.

Due to the seeds we have planted in the past, certain things are likely to happen. How we respond to those events plants new seeds. In other words, we are constantly creating our own future. If we make skillful responses, the results will be good. If we make unskillful responses, we will have a hard time in the future. We are responsible for our lives now and in the future. It is up to us. Ultimately, we can't blame anyone else. Of course we are influenced by those around us. We are influenced by our upbringing; we are influenced by many things. But nonetheless, some people have had extremely traumatic lives—terrible childhoods, dreadful experiences in relationships, but they come out of it flying. Other people have had pretty good upbringings during which nothing really horrible happened, but they ended up committing suicide. It is up to us whether we surmount our difficulties and find the way to use all that we may encounter to strengthen ourselves; or whether we go under and become embittered and obsessed with our memories, reinforcing our sense of low self-worth. Things are going to happen. What is important is how we respond.

We meet someone, and they say something to us. How we reply will condition their next remark. If we respond in a disgruntled, angry way, they will answer in a surprised and annoyed way. Tension will escalate. Then we're going to feel totally miserable and they're going be upset, too. Everything will go wrong. But if we reply in a nice and friendly way, they will surely respond in kind and then everything will unfold in a more open direction.

Far from being something very heavy and fatalistic, karma, rightly understood, expresses our total responsibility. We always have this space within which we now make a choice as to what is a skillful or unskillful response. It's not a static situation; it's not something set in concrete. Karma is constantly flowing and changing as we go in new directions, depending on how we meet the present moment. We can go up or we can go down: it is our choice. We can't put the blame on others—we can't blame our upbringing, our parents, our relationships, or the government, or the country, or the weather. It's up to us, to each one of us, moment to moment to moment. We act skillfully or we act unskillfully—the choice is ours. And that is karma, in a nutshell.

There many categories of karma: the kind of karma which operates immediately, the kind of karma which takes time, and so forth, but perhaps that's not so important here. What is important is that we understand the basic ideas behind it, and understand that karma is not fate. It's all those seeds we planted which are going to come up at some point. In every moment we plant new seeds. It's an ongoing process. That's very important to understand. Ultimately who we were in our past lives is totally irrelevant.

One time, I was staying with my aunt. When I think of the "man in the street," the ordinary person, I have to think about my family because normally I don't really meet "ordinary" people. I meet with people who are interested in spiritual matters. Actually, I think that an interest in spirituality is normal, but apparently it isn't!

In any case, my middle-aged aunt once gave a dinner party to which she invited a number of very old friends. They owned shops, or they were doctors, and so on. Just ordinary nice people. During this dinner with old friends whom she had known since adolescence, one of the men said, "I think in one of my former lifetimes I must have been Spanish, because when I went to Spain I felt this tremendous empathy with the land. I felt like I was going home even though outwardly it was a very different and alien environment." And somebody else said, "Well, that's funny, because I feel like that about Scotland. I really felt when I went there that I must have been Scottish at some time during my past lives." Soon everybody at the table began to talk about who they thought they were in their past lives, and my aunt was aghast! She'd never realized that her friends had had any thoughts of this nature.

Finally one of them turned to me and said, "Ah, but Ani-la, the question is not who we were in our past lives, is it? It's how we use *this* lifetime properly so that our future lifetimes will go well!"

That's the point. Our past lifetimes are gone, so let them go. The point is *this* lifetime—what do we do with what we have now? How do we use this life skillfully to set ourselves in the right direction, so that in future lifetimes, having planted so many good seeds in this lifetime, we can go up and up and up? That's the point.

If we see things in this way, then the adverse situations which we encounter in our life are really not problems—they are the way we learn. Of course we say this again and again, but it is so true that a nice comfortable life is very pleasant, and is obviously the result of having planted good seeds in the past. If we plant a parsnip, we get a parsnip, and if we plant a rose, we get a rose. If we plant poison ivy, we get poison ivy.

And when we reach a stretch in which everything is going very nicely—we're born in fine circumstances, things go very well for us, most of our friends are really good, we don't have too many horrible sicknesses, our families are well—that's wonderful, and very nice. But if we just stay at that level of complacency, what have we learned? How will we cope if someone close and whom we love suddenly dies, or if we contract some terrible disease? It's not that we have to go out looking for pain and problems—we're not masochists. But when problems and difficulties arise, when adverse circumstances arise, we do not try to avoid them. We take them as the path. We use them, and we realize that this is how we learn. These are the weights with which we develop our spiritual muscles.

Some people have lots and lots to learn in this lifetime. Other people seem to glide right through it. But sometimes, the people who have all the difficulties are the ones in the end who really surmount—they're the real conquerors.

It's not a matter of always trying to avoid difficulties to live in this world comfortably and nicely—that is not the objective. Animals want to be comfortable. Animals want to have food and shelter and a nice soft place to stay. Animals think mostly about food, warmth, and sex. If that's usually all that we think of, too, then we are no better than animals and that's the kind of birth we might encounter next time.

We humans share features with the animal kingdom, such as our physical body and a large part of our brain structure. But we have other qualities that animals lack. If we just let those qualities atrophy, if we let them lie in abeyance, then we're no different from animals, and this human life is wasted. We have intelligence, we have self-awareness, we have the ability to look within, we have the ability to develop genuine compassion and empathy for others. These qualities, as we develop them and as they become of paramount importance in our lives, sow so many seeds and result in so much good karma. With that, we will continue to make contact with the spiritual path and meet with spiritual masters in future lifetimes.

There are billions of people in this world. How many of them are genuinely interested in any kind of spiritual path at this point? So few. Many of them are born in countries where they are not allowed to be interested in spiritual paths. Many of them are born in countries where there are very few spiritual paths left anymore. And some of them are born in countries where there are spiritual paths and encouragement, but they have no interest.

So you are all very fortunate to be here. You are completely free, and you can believe what you like. If you want to come to a Dharma talk, you come to a Dharma talk; if you don't want to come to a Dharma talk, you don't have to come. It's up to you—it's your choice. In the West we are very lucky because although there is enormous indoctrination from the media, we don't have to buy into it.

Recently, I started to read a particular book. It concerned two visions of the future: one was the Orwellian vision, in which the whole world becomes a totalitarian state and people are subdued into conformity through fear and intimidation. The other paradigm was that of Aldous Huxley, who saw that we could be seduced by pleasure and the comfort of having everything that we want. However, when we have everything that we want and when the pleasure principle becomes paramount—that is the belief that we're in this world to be comfortable and have a nice time—then we are led into becoming like sheep, as in *Brave New World*. The author said that that is actually what is happening. People are being enticed into this whole consumer philosophy that insists that comfort and pleasure and acquisitions are the highway to eternal happiness. People buy into this ideology more and more. And that is what is helping to make us so completely soulless and spiritually flabby.

We have a choice—we can go along with that viewpoint. We can say to ourselves, "Okay. This is a good thing, so I'm going to buy more and more: a bigger house, another car, a better television, the latest computer model. That will make me happy!" We can believe that. Or we can think, "Well, I know lots of people who own those things and they're not happy. And the last time I got a better car, I was happy for two weeks but after that I wanted something else."

We may wish to consider how it is that we have this inner emptiness. Maybe trying to fill it with consumer goods and relationships isn't the answer. Perhaps there is another way in which we may genuinely fulfill and complete ourselves. So we start to look in a different direction. But that is our choice.

This is our life—we do have a choice. It is up to us whether we waste this lifetime or use it in a meaningful way that can benefit ourselves and others. Basically this is what karma is all about. Events are going to happen to us on account of actions of body, speech, and mind committed in the past. But the good news is that through our present responses, we mold our future—constantly, moment to moment to moment. We can be half-asleep or completely asleep in this moment, or we can be awake in this moment—awake, conscious, aware. The choice is ours.

Most of us actually go around half asleep. We're very busy; we're very occupied; we always have things to do. But inwardly, we're zombies. Programmed zombies—you push a button, and you get a response. Sometimes the responses are nice and sometimes they are hostile, but they're not conscious responses. That element of inner awareness, of really knowing the moment in the moment is usually not there. We're half-asleep and totally distracted.

The Buddha described three kinds of laziness. First, there is the kind of laziness we all know: we don't want to do anything, and we'd rather stay in bed half an hour later than get up and meditate. Second, there is the laziness of feeling ourselves unworthy, the laziness of thinking, "I can't do this. Other people can meditate, other people can be mindful, other people can be kind and generous in difficult situations, but I can't, because I'm too stupid." Or, alternatively, "I'm always an angry person"; "I've never been able to do anything in my life"; "I've always failed, and I'm bound to fail." This is laziness.

The third kind of laziness is being busy with worldly things. We can always fill up the vacuum of our time by keeping ever so busy. Being occupied may even make us feel virtuous. But usually it's just a way of escape. When I came out of the cave, some people said, "Don't you think that solitude was an escape?" And I said, "An escape from what?" There I was—no radio, no newspapers, no one to talk to. Where was I going to escape to? When things came up, I couldn't even telephone a friend. I was face-to-face with who I was and with who I was not. There was no escape.

Our ordinary lives are so busy, our days are so full, but we never have any space even to sit for a minute and just be. That's escape. The same aunt that I mentioned earlier always kept the radio on, or the television. She didn't like silence. Silence worried her. Background noise rang out at all times. And we're all like that. We are afraid of silence—outer silence, inner silence. When there's no noise going on outside we talk to ourselves—opinions and ideas and judgments and rehashes of what happened yesterday or during our childhood; what he said to me; what I said to him. Our fantasies, our daydreams, our hopes, our worries, our fears. There is no silence. Our noisy outer world is but a reflection of the noise inside: our incessant need to be occupied, to be doing something.

Recently I was talking with a very nice Australian monk who was once occupied with doing so many wonderful Dharma activities that he became a workaholic. He would be up until two or three in the morning. Eventually he collapsed totally. His whole system fell apart and now he can't do anything. His mind is also slightly impaired in that he doesn't have very good concentration. Of course he can talk and walk, but he can't do anything sustained in time. His problem is that his identity was connected with doing. He was really a workaholic, and as his work was for the Dharma it looked very virtuous. It looked like he was doing really good things. He was benefiting many people and carrying out the instructions of his teacher, but now that he can't do anything, who is he? And so he is going through a tremendous crisis because he always identified himself with what he did and with being able to succeed. Now he is not able to do anything and is dependent on others. So I said to him, "But this is a wonderful opportunity. Now, you don't have to do anything, you can just be." He said he was trying to come to that, but he found it very threatening not to do anything, to just sit there and be with who he is, not with what he does.

This is the point—we fill our lives with activities. Many of them are really very good activities but if we are not careful, they can just be an escape. I'm not saying that you shouldn't do good and necessary things, but there has to be breathing in as well as a breathing out. We need to have both the active and the contemplative. We need time to just be with ourselves, and to become genuinely centered, when the mind can just be quiet. Usually it's better if this is done in the early morning, because if we get up very early in the morning, provided that we haven't gone to bed too late at night, we should be fresh and bright. Usually if we get up before the rest of the household, it's more quiet. Obviously it's no good getting up to meditate when everybody else is also getting up. We have to be up before everyone else, unless others in the household are getting up and meditating too!

We know we have to make the effort. When we consider people who are dedicated to some worldly goal—athletes, artists, musicians, or whoever—anyone who is very dedicated to their particular talents works to develop their qualities with great assiduity. They give up so much time, they devote so much attention, they change their diets, they change their social habits, they give up smoking and drinking, they even sometimes give up sex, for a while at least, in order to channel all their energies into their chosen field. They dedicate themselves totally, and with total concentration, and because of that, they can hope to accomplish something.

If we seriously want to integrate the spiritual dimension with our everyday life, we have to make some sacrifices. These include getting up early so that we can have at least one half-hour or an hour of just being with ourselves and doing a serious practice, with maybe five minutes or so of generating loving-kindness for all beings at the end. Then it really changes the whole quality of the day.

As one gets used to meditation, time spontaneously begins to expand and the practice begins to influence the day. We're trying to create the circumstances through which our whole day can be used as our spiritual path. Everything we do, everybody we meet is part of practice. This is how we learn to open up our heart; this is how we open to being generous and kind, thoughtful and tolerant and patient. Understanding. More and more we become present in the moment, here and now, instead of away in cloud cuckoo land.

At the beginning we try to quiet down the tumult inside, become centered, and give ourselves some inner space so that our spiritual life and our daily life become the same thing. Outwardly, nothing has changed. But inwardly, everything has transformed.

✒ Questions

Q: If people close to you generate negative karma through their actions, can you do anything to lessen the negative karma that they create for themselves?

JTP: The Buddha actually said that we are all heirs to our own karma. However, one could do purificatory practices and keep these people in mind. For example, if one was doing Vajrasattva meditation, imagine that Vajrasattva is on their heads and purifying them also, and dedicate the merit to them. In addition, one could do positive deeds, like rescuing animals, or giving to some worthy cause, or whatever else, and dedicate the merit to them. Beyond that, there is not much we can do.

We are heirs to our own actions, and people are in that situation where they are creating their own karma. Perhaps the most we can do is give our own example. This will let them know that their conduct is not the way we think life should be led, and that what they are doing is not the kind of action of which we approve. Beyond that, what can one do? One cannot force anyone to do something if they don't want to do it. We are not responsible in that sense for others. We are responsible to our children to set them a good example, but what they do with that is up to them. Likewise with our partners or anyone else—we cannot lead their life for them. We can try to set the example of what we believe to be the right thing to do, but beyond that, whether they follow it or don't follow it, that's their responsibility, that's their choice. We do have a choice, and if they make the wrong choice then it's not our fault. Perhaps you could leave a few interesting novels of a spiritual type around the place and hope they pick them up!

People are going to do what they are going to do. All you can do from your side is to send them loving-kindness and compassion, do some purification on their behalf, and set a good example.

Q: You talked about purification. I'm really interested in the karma that I keep producing.

JTP: Are you a Buddhist of the Tibetan school? There are a number of purificatory practices in Tibetan Buddhism. For example, apart from Vajrasattva, there is the practice of Nyungné, which is a two-day fasting ritual based on the visualization of the thousand-armed Chenrezig, or Avalokiteshvara, the bodhisattva of compassion. That's very powerful for purification. But it would be difficult if you've never done it to perform it by yourself. So for that it would be good to organize a Nyungné gathering.

The prostrations to the Thirty-five Confession Buddhas is another purificatory practice. Tibetan Buddhists believe that the reason we are in such a mess and haven't realized ultimate reality yet is because of the heavy clouds of obscurations which are caused by our previous unwholesome karma. Therefore, the quickest thing to do about it is to clean up, and so there are a number of purificatory practices in order to get out the scouring brush and really get to work.

Usually, the most we can do is take a little teaspoon, but these practices are more like those big plows—snow-plows—which kind of shovel all the garbage out. If we do these practices with real conviction and with heartfelt dedication, they work very quickly. Then the signs, such as dreams, appear that we are purifying a lot of past negative karma. But of course, the important thing is not to create any further negative karma in the present.

Q: Can you be specific about abortion? For instance, if someone has had that in their past, and wants to purify that. How would you do that?

JTP: In the Tibetan tradition, there are the four powers. First is the power of remorse—we regret whatever unwholesome action we did. We genuinely regret it. It's no good thinking, for example, "Oh well, but what I did was kind of clever, and nobody else would know how to do it as well as that"—that's a kind of subtle pride in doing something which was unwholesome. And that is not regretting; there's no remorse, and then it doesn't purify. So first of all, we have to deeply regret—we are really sorry we did that action. But remorse doesn't mean that we keep on and on. There's regret, but it's not like continually picking at the scabs.

Then there is the power of reliance. That means we rely on something outside of ourselves to really help us. In this case, we rely on the purificatory practices like Vajrasattva—we believe that doing this Vajrasattva practice can really help us purify this karma.

Then we have the power of promising never to do it again. It's like we took poison, then we're really sorry we took that poison, and we vow we're definitely never going to do that again. Finally there is the power of the antidote—that means that we do something which is the opposite of what we did before. For instance, if something has been killed, we save life or we try to help children. We try to do what we can to create good karma, the direct opposite of the bad karma. If we do that with sincerity, that will help to purify.

Perhaps in the case of something like abortion, it may be a good idea on the anniversary to offer prayers for that being's good rebirth and wish him or her well on the journey through samsara. Because of course abortion is a terrible thing—we're not pretending. But also, there must have been some short life karma since the fetus of that child was born in circumstances where it couldn't come to fruition. Since then the consciousness has gone on and has taken other rebirths. So while we regret that we did what we did, still it is no good holding on. The child has gone on now. Just send prayers to wish him or her well, wherever they may be in samsara and then, as I say, do things which can compensate. For instance, if you have children, be kind to them—love them and make them know how welcome they are.

Rely on the fact that there is a way to go beyond this—it's all right. In this world of birth and death, we come into being and we go, don't we? Don't hold on to it.

Q: Is there a kind of collective karma?

JTP: No. Not from the Buddhist point of view. Anyway, collective karma is the aggregate of all the individual karmas, and if we share certain similarities, then they may come together so that we might be born in the same kind of circumstances with others of similar karmic backgrounds. I think that's what happens. But from the Buddhist point of view, there is no collective karma—that's a philosophical idea.

Q: I'll tell you what I thought in the back of my mind. It's something that comes to my mind when I'm trying to deal with cynicism. It seems to me that there has been a certain amount of spiritual progress overall. A notable example is that there is perhaps less slavery in the world today than there once was. And I find great hope and solace in the notion that we have collectively made some progress in overcoming these unwholesome practices.

JTP: You mean the world is full of remorse? There has never been such an increase in prostitution, including child prostitution, than in these days. The exploitation of human beings is ghastly. Look at the importation of these people—just recently, all those people that died in the back of the truck. And that goes on in the hundreds of cases, if not thousands and millions. And there is still slavery and bonded labor carried on in many parts of the world today.

We hope that we are progressing, but there is increasing violence, especially among the young, and there are widespread suicides. I mean, I do want to hope that we are learning our lessons, but sometimes I really wonder. I don't know if society is improving. It would be nice to think so. I'm usually surrounded by lovely people and so I get a rather rosy view of what's happening in the world. But when you look at so many countries in the world and the sheer brutality, and not just in Asia or in Africa, but in Europe and the United States, then you wonder, Are we learning anything? And so many of the young people are coming up and making exactly the same mistakes all over again—even more so sometimes.

There are wonderful people in this world, but there always were wonderful people in the world. We don't have a present-day monopoly on having saints. We don't have the monopoly on beautiful selfless people; we don't have the monopoly on having people who are looking for a genuine spiritual path. All throughout the ages, there have been people like that along with the others, and those others are still with us—our whole consumer society is based on pouring oil onto the fires of our delusion and our greed and our violence. Look at the movies.

I'm not trying to be pessimistic here. I also would like to be optimistic, and there is something in me that is optimistic, because we all have buddha nature and hopefully that will triumph. Light eventually has to triumph over darkness. Even if the darkness lasts for a million years—we switch on the light, and the light is there. The light is always there. It can never ever be destroyed. The light is the ultimate reality. But in the meantime, we are very dominated by these emotional poisons, and our society encourages that. It encourages ambition and success at the expense of others. People are becoming far more stressed-out than they ever were before. They have no time for their families; their children are neglected. The bonding which took place between people is disappearing.

Q: I was just thinking that we all have the potential to give birth to wisdom, which may compensate for the fact that yes, there are these terrible things occurring.

JTP: Yes, as I say, we all innately have the seed of buddhahood within us. That is our true nature. Our true nature is good—totally good. And in the end, that has to triumph. But it is taking a long time. Of course, in terms of eternity, this is nothing. Historical time is just a finger snap.

But that's why, from our side, we have to make the effort, because if we don't make the effort, we tend to slide downwards—at the very least into complacency—and we just try to be comfortable and to have a nice time. But that's not what this life is about. This life is really about developing spiritual muscles and doing something meaningful, not just outwardly, but inwardly. And that takes effort, because the pull of gravity is very strong. It pulls us downwards if we are not very careful. We have to be vigilant; we have to be alert. We cannot become complacent.

Q: Sometimes karma is used as a reason for not intervening in difficult situations, for example when one witnesses adults abusing children.

JTP: Well, that's the same as saying, if you've got a toothache, "Oh well, it's my karma to have a toothache so I won't go to a dentist." That's nonsense, isn't it? Maybe it's also your karma to go find a good dentist. Likewise, if someone is abusing children, then maybe it's that child's karma to find someone to help them. If you're putting karma as a reason for everything which happens then we don't do anything, do we? But nobody does that. If you're sick, you go to a doctor. You don't just sit there and say, "It's my karma."

Q: But you hear very often, "Okay, it's your karma; it's their karma."

JTP: Well maybe it is, because we've had endless lifetimes in which we've planted a million, billion seeds, both negative and positive, and you don't know when they're going to come up. But it's not what comes up which is the important thing. It's how we respond to what is happening to us. Do we respond intelligently, with skillful actions, or do we not? And just ignoring a difficult situation shows a lack of compassion, a lack of understanding, a lack of appreciation, an inability to place oneself in the shoes of another, and so forth. Clearly, if someone is suffering and one can help, then maybe it is one's karma to develop more compassion by helping.

Q: When I asked one of my lamas why the Tibetans ate meat, he pointed out to me that there were very few vegetables growing in Tibet. He said that if you ate one lettuce, how many insects were in that lettuce?

JTP: As the Buddha pointed out, this world is covered with much dust. In other words, in this realm of birth and death, things are not perfect. But there is a difference, I think, between dealing with slugs on your cabbages and with cows and sheep killed in the slaughterhouses. I think there is a level of consciousness which is rather different between a slug and a cow.

Q: What if you're in a relationship where your partner is a meat-eater and you have to prepare his food for him?

JTP: I guess you feed him meat! I know a number of people who themselves are vegetarians but cook meat for their lamas.

✍ 3
Creating Happiness

I F WE THINK of the Buddhist path as a temple, then in order to gain entry we have to go through the front door. This front door is the commitment of taking refuge. To take refuge means we are fleeing from something. What are we escaping from?

Nowadays, the world is full of refugees. Refugees are seeking refuge. They are fleeing from wars, enemies, and natural disasters that have occurred in their countries; they are escaping to some place which they hope will give safety and protection. So in Buddhism, we are all refugees. We are seeking to escape, if we have any sense, from the problems, conflicts, and difficulties of this round of birth and death. In particular, we are fleeing from conflicts which are created by our untamed, undisciplined minds, by the poisons of our delusion, greed, ill-will, pride, and jealousy, which cause so much disturbance to ourselves and to others. We are in flight from the problems of not getting what we want and getting what we don't want—old age, sickness, death. There are so many problems in this world.

Where can we find a refuge? We can find refuge only in ultimate truth. That's the only really firm ground. Nothing relative can ever be a true refuge.

It is worth noting that our consumer society always places happiness on the outside, on what we have and on what we achieve. The message is that our happiness and satisfaction rest with what we own, with what people think about us, our image. We are led to believe that if our house is bigger than our neighbor's house, or if we have more cars or a bigger television or the latest computer, this will give us a real sense of inner satisfaction, even joy. Whether you believe this or not, it's a fact that almost all of us are subject to this mentality. Even little children aren't free—when you watch children's television you see that the commercials are aimed at producing that kind of wanting, desiring mind. Because, of course, if we don't keep wanting and desiring, then we won't keep buying, and corporate profits will suffer. Purchasing is what it's all about.

Most of us have our basic needs satisfied. We have somewhere to live; we have clothing to cover us; we have sufficient food. Actually, our needs are very small. And yet we pass beyond our needs into greed, into artificial desires which are continually being stimulated by our society. And the majority of people fall for it. They really believe that if they have a bigger, better house or a bigger, better car, or a more interesting and attractive partner, then they will have reached nirvana! We do feel this, especially the bit about the partner. We think that if we could just find the ideal relationship with that perfect person who does exactly what we want them to do and is totally satisfying to us in every way, we would be perfectly happy. This is very telling.

We're like hamsters in a wheel. We're constantly running on this treadmill, working hard and exhausting ourselves but getting absolutely nowhere, because no matter what we have, there's always something else more. The majority of the world goes for it: we believe that if we only had whatever it is that we desire, we would finally be satisfied.

In the Buddhist tradition, we regard as a refuge the Buddha, his teachings, and the community of those who have realized those teachings. Why? The Buddha was a prince who had everything he wanted. He had three palaces for the three seasons of the year, he had doting parents, a beautiful wife, and he even had a son. He was very handsome, athletic, and intelligent. He had lots of wealth, slaves and servants, concubines, silks, gold and jewels, and everything else a prince could possibly want. Outwardly he had everything. So why did he leave home searching for the cause of his dissatisfaction?

During outings when he had left the palace, he beheld the spectacle of a very old man, a sick man, and finally, a corpse. This was a great revelation for him, because these things had been hidden from him during his life of indulgence. Maybe they were not physically hidden from him, but he had not really thought about these things.

While we are young we usually don't think of old age, sickness, and death. Those things happen to those old fogies elsewhere. We don't think that inevitably they will happen to us. The Buddha left home because he had experienced that life is not the way it always appears to be. The Buddha started from where we are.

We think of life as something pretty static, fairly secure. We're always trying to keep what we have, keep our relationships the way they are, stay looking much the way we did when we were in our prime. We deny the very real facts of change and impermanence, that everything changes moment to moment—the cells in our body, the thoughts in our mind. Everything everywhere in every moment is in a state of flux. But we try to hold on. We continually deny the fact that everything is changing, everything is flowing, and that meetings end in partings.

When the Buddha was enlightened in northern India 2500 years ago, he realized his full human potential, a potential that we all possess but which is normally closed to us. It wasn't that he was a god—he was a human being. After his enlightenment, he set off on foot and traveled to Benares, now called Varanasi. Outside Varanasi there is a small park, Deer Park, and here he met with his five erstwhile companions who had left him after he had given up extreme austerity and had begun to eat again. He taught what is called "The First Sermon," or in Buddhist terms, he first turned the Wheel of the Dharma. And what did he teach as the quintessence of his understanding of his enlightenment? He didn't talk about joy and love and light. He talked about suffering. He talked about the basic unsatisfactory nature of our existence as we normally lead it. The Buddha started right where we are, and said that the ordinary life of an ordinary person is in a state of dis-ease. Somehow, it's never quite right. Sometimes it's extremely wrong, and sometimes it's almost right, but it's never *exactly* right.

Basic dissatisfaction runs through all our lives, and the Buddha called this *dukkha*. It comes in many forms, of course, from gross physical suffering to emotional and mental pain, to spiritual suffering. There are so many forms of this sense of unease because we have been on this planet for thousands of years. Almost everyone wants to be happy, not just human beings: animals, insects, all sentient life basically wants to be happy. When most people open their eyes in the morning, they don't wake up and think, "How can I be as miserable as possible today and make everybody else miserable too?" Some people might, but the majority don't.

We'd all like to be happy. And we expend a great deal of effort trying to make ourselves happy. Through the centuries people have pondered this dilemma of how to be happy and stay happy. So how is it that most people are so unhappy? Not only are they miserable, but they make the people around them miserable, too. Many people have a great deal of pain in their lives, which they try to alleviate in whatever way they can. Others, however, on the surface at least, feel quite content with their lot. The issue of contentment is a very important one.

After his enlightenment, the Buddha started teaching from exactly where we are. He said, "Life the way we lead it is not satisfying. There is an inner lack, an inner emptiness, an inner sense of meaninglessness which we can't fill with things or people. What is the cause of this inherent unrest, this inherent sense of dissatisfaction which eats at us?"

The Buddha taught that the essential reason for this dis-ease within us is our grasping, desiring mind, which is based on our essential ignorance. Ignorance of what? Basically, the ignorance of understanding the way things really are. That can be explored on many levels, but we'll deal with it first of all from the point of view that not only do we not recognize impermanence, we also don't recognize our genuine nature. Therefore, we're always grasping outwards. We don't realize our inner interconnection, and we identify always with this sense of self and other.

Now, as soon as we have the idea of self and other, we therefore have the idea of wanting to acquire that which is attractive and to push away that which we want to avoid. Then this sense of inner emptiness has to be filled up, and we give in to grasping, clinging, and attachment. And of course we think in our delusion that our grasping, clinging mind, our attachment to things and to people, is what will bring us happiness. We do it all the time. We're attached to our possessions; we're attached to the people we love; we're attached to our position in the world, and to our career and to what we have attained. We think that holding on to these things and to these people tightly will give us security, and that security will give us happiness. That is our fundamental delusion, because it's the very clinging which makes us insecure, and that insecurity which gives us this sense of dis-ease, this unease.

Nobody binds us with chains to this wheel. We clasp it; we grip it with all our might. The way to get off the wheel is to let go. Do you understand? That grasping, clinging mind is the cause of our suffering, but we're very deluded because we think that our greed and our lusts and our desires point toward the sources of happiness. However much we deny it, we really believe that somehow or other, if all our wants are fulfilled, we will be happy. But the fact is that our wants can never all be fulfilled. Wants are endless. The Buddha said that it was like drinking salty water—we just get more and more thirsty.

What does Buddhism mean by non-attachment? Many people think the idea of detachment, non-attachment, or non-clinging is very cold. This is because they confuse attachment with love. But attachment isn't genuine love—it's just self-love.

When I was eighteen, I told my mother I was going to India. I remember I met her on the street as she was coming home from work and said, "Oh, Mum, guess what? I'm going to India!"

And she replied, "Oh yes, dear. When are you leaving?"

She said that not because she didn't love me, but because she did love me. She loved me so much that she wanted me to be happy. Her happiness lay in my happiness, and not in what I could do to make her happy.

Non-attachment doesn't have anything to do with what we own or don't own. It's just the difference between whether the possessions own us or whether we own the possessions. There is a story of a king in ancient India. He had a palace, concubines, gold, silver, jewels, silks, and all the nice things that kings have. He also had a brahmin guru, who was extremely ascetic. All that this brahmin owned was a clay bowl, which he used as a begging bowl.

One day, the king and his guru were sitting under a tree in the garden when the servants came running up and cried, "Oh Maharaja, Your Majesty, come quickly, the whole palace is in flames! Please come quickly!"

The king replied, "Don't bother me now—I'm studying the Dharma with my guru. You go and deal with the fire."

But the guru jumped up and cried, "What do you mean? I left my bowl in the palace!"

What we're talking about is the mind. We're not talking about possessions. Possessions and things are innocent; they are not the problem. It doesn't matter how much we own or what we don't own: it's our attachment to what we own which is the problem. If we lose everything tomorrow and say, "Oh there we are, easy come and easy go," there's no problem; we're not caught. But if we are distressed, that is a problem.

Clinging to things and to people reveals our fear of losing them. And when we do lose them, we grieve. Instead of holding things so tightly, we can hold them more lightly. Then while we have these things, while we have these relationships, we enjoy them. We treasure them. But if they go, well, that's the flow of things. When there is no hope or fear in the mind, the mind is free. It's our greedy, grasping mind that is the problem.

There's a story about a kind of monkey trap which they use in Asia. It's a hollowed-out coconut which is nailed to a tree or a stake. This coconut has a little hole in it just big enough for a monkey to put his hand in, and inside the coconut they put something sweet. And so the monkey comes along, smells the bait, puts his hand into the hole, and grasps the sweet. So now he has a fist holding the sweet. But when he tries to withdraw his fist through the hole, he can't. So he's caught. And then the hunters come and just pick him up.

Nothing is holding that monkey to the coconut. He could just let go of the sweet and be out and away. But the greed in his mind, even with his fear of the hunters, will not let him let go. He wants to go, but he also wants to have the sweet. And that's our predicament. Nothing but our insecure and grasping mind is holding us to our hopes and fears. This is a very fundamental and important point, because we are trained to think that satisfying our desires is the way to happiness. Actually, to go beyond desire is the way to happiness. Even in relationships, if we're not holding on, if we're not clinging, if we are thinking more of how we can give joy to the other rather than how they can give joy to us, then that also makes our relationships much more open and spacious, much more free. All that jealousy and fear are gone.

In the East, no one ever asked me, "Why on earth did you go live in a cave?" Only in the West do people ask that question. To an Asian, it's obvious. But because our society fantasizes this glamour of success and wealth, having so much and so many possessions, our whole psyche becomes distorted. We are continually creating this outer glittering image which has little connection with what's going on inside that image. It's just the external manifestation of success. I have met a number of very wealthy, successful, and famous people, but they were not particularly happy people. They might be the envy of many, but actually they came to talk to me about all their problems.

We live in our mind. We spend so much time buying nice houses, decorating them according to our desires, making everything look very nice. We keep them clean, well-furnished, and beautifully decorated, and we show them with pride to other people. But actually, we don't live in our houses, we live in our minds. We also spend a lot of time on our physical appearance, always trying to look young and attractive, to wear the right kind of clothes and give people the right kind of impression. We think, "This is who I am."

If we go somewhere else, we leave our house behind. We don't carry it with us; we are not snails. But our mind we carry with us everywhere; we live within our minds. Everything we see is projected to us through our five senses organs which impinge on our consciousness and then are interpreted by the mind. The mind itself is considered as the sixth sense: one which is constantly churning up memories, thoughts, ideas, opinions, judgments, likes, and dislikes. We live inside our mind. Where else do we live? If we go to Europe, if we go to Africa, if we go to Asia, we take our mind with us. Whether we are in the middle of Sydney or up the mountain in a cave, we bring our mind with us. This is where we live, we live in our mind.

But how many of us take the trouble to decorate our minds? When we consider the amount of input—television, movies, magazines, newspapers, and all the cacophony with which we live constantly—this junk is being poured into our mind every waking minute, and we never empty it out. It's like a great big garbage pit in there. Think of it. All this trash is constantly being shoveled into our minds and we never get rid of it: it's all in there. Sometimes I think it would be interesting to have a loud-speaker attached to our minds so everyone would hear what we are constantly thinking. Wouldn't we all want to learn to meditate quickly, quickly? We'd all want to learn how to control our wild mind and deal with all the junk in there.

Now, would you invite the Dalai Lama into your home if it was full of junk and garbage and hadn't ever been cleared out? You wouldn't. You would clean it first. You would make it nice and have everything beautifully arranged, open all the doors and windows to let fresh air in and then you would invite His Holiness into your house.

So how can we invite wisdom into a mind which is just a cesspool? Seriously. First, we have to do a bit of cleaning up. We have to open up the doors and windows to let some fresh air in. Initially, that's what this whole question of meditation and learning how to be present in the moment and such practices are all about. They're about learning how to cleanse the mind, because even if we just cleaned the windows a bit, we could see out. Now, we see everything through our confused, turbulent minds full of the poisons of ill-will, greed, delusion and so on. No wonder we're confused. As I keep saying, we want to be happy, so why do we keep doing things which create the opposite? Why? We want to be happy, we want to make others happy, we put effort into it, so how is it that we're not all radiantly blissful?

There is a state of mind beyond suffering, a state of mind which is free. Even in our own way, as ordinary people, we can begin to incorporate some of these qualities—like generosity and compassion—into our life. It's not as impossible as it might sound. But first, to see how we create our own suffering, we have to understand that opening to such qualities is necessary, and we have to understand why it's necessary. Our suffering doesn't depend on what is happening "out there." It really depends on our own mind, the state of our own mind, and our reactions to what is happening out there.

People who are mentally disturbed spend a lot of time thinking about themselves; they're obsessed with their own happiness and their own suffering and they spend much time, as many of us do, on wondering, "How can I be happy?" But the irony of the situation is that, if we think less about how we can make ourselves happy, and more about how we can make others happy, somehow we end up being happy ourselves. People who are genuinely concerned with others have a much happier and more peaceful state of mind than those who are continually trying to manufacture their own joys and satisfactions.

We are basically very selfish people. When anything happens, our very first thought is, "How will this affect *me?*" Think about it. "What's in it for *me?*" If it doesn't negatively affect oneself, then it's all right, and we don't care. This very self-centered way of viewing the world is one of the principal causes of our unrest, because the world is the way it is; the world is never going to fit into all our expectations and our unrealistic hopes.

We have this human potential—our great human potential—to go beyond that to something much more profound which will give us genuine inner calm, not just superficial physical pleasure, but genuine, profound, deep, lasting happiness. It is within us; it is not "out there." A mind which is more peaceful, more centered, and which is able to hold things lightly, which is not always grasping, which is not constantly churned on the waves of our hopes and our fears; a mind which is settled, which sees things clearly and with a heart which is open toward others, is a happy mind. And that happiness doesn't depend on external circumstances. That mind is able to ride the waves of our external pains and pleasures. The answer lies within us.

I met a man in Australia who was dying of leukemia; he was like a skeleton. In fact, he died the day after I visited him. He was in his fifties. Before going to meet him, I met with members of his family. His wife said to me, "Could you ask him about his funeral arrangements?"

"Haven't you discussed this?" I asked.

"Oh no, no," she said. "We can't discuss death."

His mother and father, who had just celebrated their ninetieth birthdays, exclaimed, "How could this happen to us?"

I pointed out the hospital window. "Excuse me?" I said. Crowds of people were going backwards and forwards. "You find me one person out there who hasn't lost someone that they loved. What do you mean, 'How could this happen to us?' Why shouldn't it happen to you? It happens to everybody else."

It is denial. We celebrate birth with dancing but we absolutely shuffle our feet when it comes to acknowledging death. Yet all of our life is a preparation for dying. If we were going to die tonight, what would we do now, right now? We're all of us on a train and that train is going to crash for sure, so how are we going to spend the journey?

At the time of death, do you want to die thinking, "What did I do with my life?" or, "Why have I wasted my life?" So often we plan, "Oh, I'll start to practice when the kids get older and leave home," or, "I'll start to practice when I retire." Who knows if we're going to be around that long?

The Buddha said that the one thing certain about life is death. That is true. It doesn't matter how old or how young we are. I'm sure all of us have friends who were very young when they met with some tragic accident or developed some fatal disease. Who would have expected them to die? Today we are here, and tomorrow we are gone. We can't think, "I'm going to live for three score years and ten and then I'll die." Who knows when we are going to die? Just because we are young and healthy today doesn't mean we are not going to be dead tomorrow. We don't know; none of us knows.

Once, not so long ago, I went to a meeting with other participants very early one morning. As we drove along in the early light we saw a crowd of school-children by a school bus. They were all standing around, looking completely dazed. A woman was lying dead in the middle of the street. She had just been hit; she wasn't covered up. She was a young woman, maybe in her thirties, wearing a gray top and faded jeans. It was quiet and the ambulance had not yet arrived. The accident had only just happened. The bus driver hadn't seen her as she crossed the road.

If we knew we were going to die tomorrow—and we don't know that we're *not* going to die tomorrow—what would we do today? How would we spend our time? What would we do with our body; what would we do with our speech; what would we do with our mind?

The word *buddha* means "to be awake" and is the culmination of ultimate wisdom, compassion, and purity. We go for refuge to that. We go for refuge to our own inner potential for buddhahood. We all possess what is called buddha nature. That means we all possess within ourselves the fullness of wisdom, compassion, and purity. But it is covered over. And it is this which connects us with all beings—not just human beings, but animals, insects and everything that is sentient. Anything which has consciousness has this potential. It might take a long time to uncover it, or it might happen in a moment, but we have it. We also go for refuge to that within ourselves—our own innate true nature.

When we go for refuge to the Dharma, first of all we go for refuge to the teachings of the Buddha. After the Buddha's enlightenment, he went around northeast India for forty-five years talking to many different sorts of people— the rich and the poor, lay people and monks, males, females, the young and old—and much of this instruction was recorded. In the Tibetan canon, there are one hundred and eight volumes of the Buddha's teachings. But we also go for refuge to the Dharma in the sense of ultimate reality—to that which is revealed when the clouds of our confusion and delusion part and we see truth face-to-face. That ultimate reality is out there and within ourselves, too. That is the true Dharma, the universal law.

The meaning of *sangha*, or community, is threefold. There are the ordained monks and nuns who are the monastic sangha. Then there is the *maha*, or great, sangha—that means all followers, monastic or lay, of the Buddha. Lastly there is the *arya*, or noble, sangha, who are those, monastic or lay, who have had authentic experience and realizations of the nature of reality. This last category is the genuine sangha refuge.

It is as if we are all sick. Sick with the five poisons of delusion, greed, ill will, pride, and envy. The Buddha is like a physician who says, "You're sick but you can be cured," and then he prescribes the medicine. The medicine is the Dharma. And just as with ordinary medicine, it is no good just reading the label or knowing the ingredients: we have to take the medicine; we have to follow the cure. And there is a cure. We can be healed. Those who help us and look after us are the sangha. They are like nurses—they take care of us, they help us to take the medicine in the right doses, they look after us until we are completely healed. When we are healed, we can then take their place and help others.

Genuine happiness comes from the heart. It comes from a mind which has become more stable, more clear, more present in the moment; a mind which is open and cares for the happiness of other beings. It is a mind which has that inner security, a knowing that whatever happens can be handled. It is a mind that doesn't hold on so tightly any more; it is a mind that holds things lightly. This kind of mind is a happy mind.

Let us take His Holiness the Dalai Lama as an example. He lost his country. Every day people come to him from Tibet and elsewhere with ghastly stories. Truly awful things are happening in Tibet. He sees his people suffering. And not only that: because of his position, people come from all over the world to tell him of oppression in their own countries. He takes it all completely to heart. When people tell him of their sufferings, he weeps. But when you think of His Holiness, you think of him as always smiling and happy. You look into his eyes and they're dancing. Why?

When people are in the presence of His Holiness they are so happy, and they come out floating. It's because he has this quality of genuinely caring for others beyond himself. He has this quality of really putting the happiness of others before himself so that for everyone he meets—president or Pope or road-worker, it doesn't matter—his only thought is that they should be happy. It doesn't matter who they are. It doesn't matter whether on one level he might or might not like them. His only concern is for their happiness and well-being. He is concerned with the real person, not the mask, not the glittering image these people are wearing. He is concerned with the real person. When looking at that person his only thought is to wish them well. We can all do this.

The ceremony of taking refuge comes from the time of the Buddha himself. When the Buddha was wandering around in northern India he met so many people seeking his advice. At the end of many of these discourses in the sutras, the questioner states, "From now until life's end, I take refuge in the Buddha, in the Dharma, in the Sangha." It is a very ancient tradition in all Buddhist countries. It expresses commitment to put the spiritual path in the center of our life instead of just at the periphery. It is a commitment which says, "From now on, I will transform my life into something meaningful." Therefore, taking refuge is the beginning of the Buddhist path.

Toward every person we meet, starting with those who are the closest to us—our families, our colleagues, people that we meet everyday, and then extending that to strangers and whomever else we meet—our first thought should be the appreciation that they want happiness. They aren't just anonymous blobs: they're people with problems, with pleasures and pains. They want to be happy, just as we want to be happy. Cultivating that attitude toward everyone breaks down the ego-centered selfishness which causes us so much pain. So long as we are fixated on ourselves, on how we can be happy, we will never be happy. It is only when we open up our hearts to include all beings that suddenly we discover there is this inner joy within us: it begins like a little spring of water and is without the dryness of our self-cherishing thoughts. As our essential nature is love and intelligence, we are not inherently bad. We are inherently perfect. It is just that this nature has become covered over, like the sun covered by thick clouds. We may identify ourselves with the clouds because we don't see the sun. But the sun is always there.

These qualities will become stronger and stronger once we begin to practice. As long as we rely on things or on other people for our happiness, we will never genuinely be satisfied, because these things are impermanent. They're transient; they're insecure.

The only true happiness lies within us. That's where it is.

✍ Questions

Q: What was your central motivation for spending so many years in the cave in the Himalayas?
JTP: My motivation? The Dharma in itself is motivating. Once you realize the benefits of practice, then it keeps you going. It becomes more and more central; it takes over your life, as you can see! But in recent years, my motivation has been very much to help young women from the Buddhist Himalayan regions who want to devote their lives to the Dharma. One sees that they have such incredible intelligence; they have such a spark, and one wants to help them. If we don't help them, who will?

Q: Is it true that nuns are not educated in the Tibetan Buddhist culture? And can you tell us about the nunnery you have started in northern India?
JTP: You know, you are really very fortunate in the West. You are all well-educated and you can read whatever you want. You can study whatever you want to study and if any spiritual teachers come, you can go and listen to them without obstacles. Basically, you're very free.

I think it's hard for people in the West to appreciate a society where there are obstacles to being able to study. For example, in the Himalayan regions like Ladakh and Bhutan, there are many monks and nuns. But, there is no education for the nuns. When I lived in Lahaul, I saw this very clearly. While the monks were benefiting from doing the rituals, receiving the teachings, and going into long retreats, the nuns were in the kitchen doing the cooking.

Recently, I saw a video filmed in Ladakh. There was one Ladakhi nun who stated, after a week's course of teachings on monastic rules for the nuns, "I've been a nun for forty years and this is the first teaching I've ever received." You have to understand where these people are coming from. The nuns in these Himalayan regions especially and in Tibet are often basically just ser-vants for their families or for the monks. Previously, the nuns were not very well educated. They often did do some practice, but of course now, with the Communist takeover, even that is very much curtailed. So hundreds of nuns are fleeing into India constantly from Tibet even at the present time.

What we're trying to do is create opportunities for these girls to realize both their intellectual and their spiritual potential. To me, so many of these girls are like tight little buds. As they grow old and die they're just withered buds because they've never had any sunshine, no rain, no fertilizer, nothing. We're trying to give them the sunshine, fertilizer, and rain of our approval so they can study and practice. They are already doing that! They are so enthusiastic, so keen; they're like dry little sponges which hungrily absorb everything we teach them. They can't get enough.

The thing is, there are hundreds or maybe thousands of girls who have been denied the opportunity of realizing their spiritual potential. Now, we are trying to rectify this by giving them the opportunity to be able to study and practice as the monks have been doing for centuries.

Q: How are nuns formally ordained in your tradition?
JTP: It's a little bit esoteric. There's no full ordination. As far as we know, no fully ordained nuns ever went to Tibet from India, so the bhikshuni ordina-tion was never taken to Tibet. Now, they are trying to introduce this ordina-tion via the Chinese tradition but there are some complications. Only a few Tibetan nuns have traveled abroad to receive the bhikshuni ordination, since the Chinese follow a different ordination lineage.

The problem is that at the moment it's usually the younger nuns who go to take the ordination. When they return to their nunneries as fully ordained nuns, the older nuns who have a lower ordination are nonetheless senior to them. There are a lot of problems in that. What I'm trying to do in my nun-nery is ensure that the nuns take their ordination in order. In a few years' time, when they're ready, we'll get the whole first lot ordained together so they'll be not only senior in age and experience but also senior in ordination. I think that's the way it has to go.

Q: Can lay people also gain realization?
JTP: Of course, one doesn't have to be a monk or a nun in order to attain realization. In Tibet, for example, some of the very greatest spiritual masters were lay people. It certainly isn't a prerequisite to enter the sangha. However, any kind of realization takes great dedication and the lay life is more distracting. It's much more of a challenge to keep one's focus. Also, because realization does depend on the question of non-attachment and non-grasping, it's much more difficult in a lay situation. But nonetheless, the nature of the mind is the nature of the mind whether you're a monk or a lay person. It's there to be realized.

Q: What is the role of compassion in the spiritual path, and how can a lay person practice it?
JTP: Compassion is extraordinarily important in the spiritual path. It's the other side of the coin: we have both wisdom and compassion. The greater the understanding of the inherent pain in beings—the more the mind becomes very clear, as if wiping away dust from the eyes—the more one sees the underlying pain in people's lives, and the more compassion arises. Even if overtly people don't look like they are suffering, we see that under the façade there is a lot of pain and many problems. Naturally then compassion arises, and the two feed each other. Compassion without wisdom is sterile; it is blind. It's like having legs but no eyes. Wisdom without compassion is like being crippled; you can't go anywhere. So, we need the two, and they mutually support each other because it's not just that the intellect has to be open, the heart also has to be open. They are indivisible. Wisdom and compassion are like two wings. We cannot fly with one alone.

Q: Many Western Buddhists have family and friends who are not open to Buddhist philosophy when it's presented within the dogmatic or cultural trappings. How do you bring Buddhist concepts and methods to those who might be put off by an explicitly Buddhist approach to life?
JTP: The point is that we are not all trying to become Tibetans or Japanese. What we are trying to do is become better people. So without any of the Bud-

dhist jargon, if you are becoming a kinder, more thoughtful, more generous, more centered person, then people will look at that and think, well this looks like a good thing. It really works. This person is not nearly as irritable and selfish as they used to be, they are much more thoughtful, they're much more kind, they're much more peaceful, this must be a good thing. That's the best way to teach Buddhism. Not through jargon, but through example.

Q: That's why many Westerners are attracted to this Buddhist philosophy and these schools of Buddhism. But there are also these very strong religious aspects. You can make a choice if you want to be very religious.

JTP: Yes, but you can do that behind your own closed doors, you don't have to go around stinking of religion. Private devotions are private. Outside, you should try to blend with your society while remaining centered and mindful and more kind and generous. The practice is bearing fruit once we begin to overcome our negative emotions and cultivate the positive.

Q: There is a lot of work to do.

JTP: A lot of work. And where better to start than with your family and with your friends who don't believe you anyway! Fortunately, in Buddhism we don't have to convert people. People respect the Buddhadharma through the examples of the Buddhists that they meet.

ೞ 4
The Eight Worldly Concerns

W E ARE NOT generally aware of our appetite for praise and our dread of blame. We are not generally aware of how we yearn for a good reputation and fall anxious at the thought of the bad. We are not generally aware of the urgency of our desire for gain and our fear of loss. We are not generally aware of how much we gravitate toward what we regard as pleasurable, nor how much we try to avoid what we regard as painful. But it is these eight worldly concerns that keep us revolving around and around in this cycle of birth and death, samsara.

The eight worldly concerns condition a great part of what we do and what we plan. They may even condition our spiritual practice. What underlies our reaching out for what seems good and pleasurable and this avoidance of what is not? What are we really looking for? What sort of peace do we hope to gain?

We may hope to gain something, something from all the effort we put into trying to get and trying to avoid, but the very grasping that underlies our effort is precisely what holds us to this whole cycle of birth and death. We may even regard such grasping as pleasurable. This dynamic of motivation, of desire and aversion, hope and fear, keeps our ordinary egoistic preoccupations going. And we are not even conscious of it. We assume it's natural that we want pleasure and don't want pain; we assume it's natural to hope for gain and to fear loss. We don't question the very structure of this dualistic mindset, which is based on ignorance of our situation.

Buddhism inquires into this underlying ignorance of our true identity. Attending to whatever, even sitting with this book in hand, we may have a very solid sense of *I* around which the rest of the world revolves. It is so habitual, we don't even notice it.

I and *mine*; *I* and *me*; *my family*; *my children*; *my partner*; *my* whatever. This sense of *I* is very solid, real, and enduring. It is something that is deeply formed within us, and as our society mirrors this solidity, we don't question it: *Of course I exist. Here I am. I must exist exactly the way I appear to exist.* We come early to this notion, which from the Buddhist point of view is regarded as *avidya*, deeply ingrained unknowing. In Sanskrit, *vidya* means to know; *avidya* means to not know. This very deeply rooted tendency to not see things as they are is something we share with practically everybody we meet. And we think our viewpoint must be true because it reflects how everybody sees one another.

This solid sense of *I* is what we project onto others; it is what others mirror back to us. It is how we see ourselves when we look at ourselves. It is a very deeply ingrained unknowing.

We identify ourselves with so many things. We identify with our bodies, our race, our nationality, our gender, our profession, our relationships. We identify ourselves as the child of certain parents, and perhaps even as a parent ourselves. We identify ourselves as someone's partner, or as someone's sibling. *This is who I am.* And identification doesn't stop there. We identify with our memories, too. Our memories concretize our sense of self. "Oh no," we may think, as someone else recalls some shared experience, "it wasn't like that at all."

We believe our opinions. We believe our prejudices. We believe in ourselves as a solid and separate individual: me. *I think this; I think that; in my opinion . . .* We do it automatically.

This sense of *I*, of a *me* separate from everything else which is not me, which is other, is an expression of our primordial ignorance from a Buddhist point of view. All Buddhist practices are directed to overcoming such notions so that we may open up to a level of being that is much vaster than this tiny little ego we cling to so desperately. Clinging to this sense of *I* we reach out through our greed and grasping for anything that will give apparent pleasure to this ego. At the same time, we try to push away anything that will give it pain. Aversion finds expression through anger, aggression, and negativity. We do it automatically. Maybe it is stirring in you now.

You sit on your cushion with an aim to have a nice meditation session, and in the beginning it is quite comfortable. After a bit, your knees start to hurt, and your back, and automatically you move to avoid the pain and bring back the pleasure, the comfort. Bringing desire and aversion even to our spiritual practice, we try to avoid anything which is not physically or mentally comfortable. Even though we may seem to be sitting on our cushion, we are tossed by the waves of samsara.

It is the nature of waves to go up and come down. But of course if you go and cling to the idea of going up, you must also accept the fact that you will come down.

Everything is impermanent. From moment to moment change reveals itself. Though we try endlessly to negotiate, something always seems to come along to smash whatever it is that we cling to. Endlessly, frantically, we try to get it back again. Our lives unfold like this. And it is so normal we don't question it. But until we begin to question it, until we begin to become more conscious of how we engage in this struggle all of the time, we cannot open to inner equanimity.

The eight worldly concerns—maybe we should call them the eight worldly hang-ups! Hung up on them, our mind can't get free. We hope everything will work out; we fear that so much will not work out. But this kind of security is elusive. Samsara by its very nature is not secure. So long as we try to make everything fit our ideas of how everything should be, how everything should go along, we are caught. And there is always something: haven't you noticed? The world around you may never seem quite right, or else it is right just for a second, until something else happens. *Everything would be fine, if only... * But there is always an *if only.*

Running a nunnery, I am very conscious of this. Every morning I wake up and wonder, What will it be today? We can spend our lives worrying like this, caught between our desire for things to go as we want and resisting the way they go anyway. Or we can develop the inner ability to know that this process is happening within us: we can become like a boat, just riding the waves of samsara. We can open to equanimity as we deal with situations. However much we want to gain acknowledgment, pleasure, praise, reputation—the fact of the matter is that we gain some and we lose some. Sometimes things are difficult for us. Sometimes we suffer. We experience criticism, obscurity, discomfort, pain. We lose things. We lose people. We lose our health, and eventually we lose our precious life.

We suffer when we live our lives as a form of resistance against things not going as we want. We suffer when we try desperately to make things go exactly as we plan and they don't. This is the point. The Buddha said there are two kinds of suffering: there is physical suffering and mental suffering.

Physical suffering we can't avoid. Even the Buddha himself had physical suffering. Everybody—as you see if you live long enough—has aches and pains and accidents and sometimes very serious illnesses.

We have a body, and our body is going to deteriorate. It is inevitable. But what is not inevitable is mental suffering, and in this we have a say. We can train our mind so that even if the body suffers the mind does not. When we are sick, or when things go wrong, we can go down in despair or we can maintain our equanimity. It is crucial that we appreciate just why this is important. Because when things go well, we often think everything is fine and that there is no real need to do much. But when things fall apart, what will we do? Today we are fine, tomorrow we may have a serious accident. Today we are with the person we love most, tomorrow they are gone.

In Buddhism there are considered to be many higher levels of rebirth: twenty-six different levels of celestial rebirth where everything goes according to how we want it. The eight worldly dharmas do not really exist through these levels, as you just have to think of something and it appears. Going up to higher and higher levels of being, finally there are just mental levels with no bodies. One has a body of light, and everything is very joyful, very pleasurable. But all of these heavenly levels, which are the result of very good karma, are regarded from a Buddhist perspective as being a spiritual dead end because there is no incentive to practice. And as the length of life is very, very long in such realms, there is no thought of death and impermanence; there is no thought of suffering; there is no thought about anything, really. There is just the enjoyment of good karma's results. So that might all be very nice, and in many spiritual traditions people aim to get reborn there, but of course from a Buddhist perspective these twenty-six levels of celestial rebirth are impermanent.

And there is the matter of the hell realms, where the suffering is so intense and unremitting that one is totally closed within one's own fear and pain, unable to think beyond one's own distress. But the hell realms, too, are impermanent.

Human birth is ideal because we all have this time within which to practice. Nice things keep us going; difficult things act as incentives. The point therefore is that we need to take the life we have—right now—and look at it. Look at how we are living it.

What are you actually doing with your precious life?

You are very well endowed. You are educated; you live in a society in which you can think what you want to think; and you can do more or less what you want to do. If you want to read certain books, not only can you read them, you can understand them. This is very rare in this world.

One of our nunnery's teachers recently came back from a tour of Europe—eleven countries in nineteen days, and how he loved it! What he especially noticed was how clean everything is, and how all the drivers, although there are so many cars, drive in their own lanes. He was amazed! Nobody constantly blared their horns; no cows wandered the roads. Coming to the West from one of the many depressed countries of the world is really like coming to heaven. This is why people want to come. Because however difficult their circumstances when they arrive, the West is still an incredible place compared with what they have left. There is so much opportunity to go forward. You live in a blessed situation already.

You have the opportunity to work on your mind. You are not endlessly thinking about where you can find the next meal for your children. You have the leisure and the opportunity to think beyond that. You will never get a better time than right now to use this life meaningfully. The eight worldly concerns—praise/blame, good reputation/bad reputation, gain/loss, pleasure/pain—offer us profound questions to explore within ourselves. Accordingly, we can spend our whole lives integrating what we find.

Modern life is stressful. But we add to this stress continually. Most people are consumed by worries, and yet most of these worries are really not necessary. We have anxieties about the future, but the future has not come. What about right now? Right now we are just sitting. We might not be very comfortable, but at least we are sitting and nobody is threatening us and it is fairly okay! So what is there to worry about? Ninety percent of what we worry about doesn't happen anyway.

This doesn't mean that we can't plan, but once having planned for something, the skillful thing is to let it go. And open up to accept whatever happens, because that is simply what is happening in the moment. We have this idea that if things go the way we want them to go and are pleasurable and nice, then that is a good thing for us and proves our success. If things go wrong for us and are painful or difficult, we imagine this as a sign of our failure. Samsara, we think, ought to be happy. But the Buddha said that samsara is unsatisfactory.

The point is not the loss and pain and criticism. The point is our aversion to that. We think we shouldn't have to experience loss; we think we shouldn't have to experience pain; we think we shouldn't have to experience criticism. But the loss and pain and criticism are just how things are. Everybody has some pleasure and some pain. Everybody has some people saying nice things and some people saying bad things about them. But that is not the problem. The problem is that we resent and resist anything which the ego considers to be unpleasant. And we cling to and attach ourselves very strongly to anything that would give pleasure to this sense of *me*. But if we just open ourselves to accept whatever is happening as it is actually happening in the moment, there is no problem. Our anxieties fade.

We take the eight worldly concerns with us everywhere. They are finely woven into the fabric of our minds. We meet them in daily life in our workplace, in our relationships with our friends, and at home with our family. They come with us into Dharma centers, too, very much so. This is what Chögyam Trungpa Rinpoche referred to, of course, as spiritual materialism.

Egoism can easily take hold of our spiritual practice. We may study the Dharma, do practices, and go to teachings and retreats, but all can become means to enhance this sense of I: *I am a spiritual person; I have read so many Buddhist books; I have met all the best lamas; I have received all the main empowerments; I do important things at my Dharma center; I am special.* It really is up to us to question and honestly look at our mind. One Catholic priest I know said that we are like pieces of rough wood. If we always stroke ourselves with silks and velvet, that's very nice, but we don't become smooth. In order to become smooth, you need sandpaper. The so-called difficulties and problems that we meet with in our daily lives are as sandpaper and make us smooth. This is how we learn. This is how we really measure ourselves and grow up.

Underneath, we can see how intolerant we are toward ourselves. Caught by our self-judgments and prejudices, we have this picture of how we should be. But when things don't fit in, this creates a lot of distress, anxiety, and tension. A lot of desire and aversion, hope and fear.

Instead of being swept up by the eight worldly concerns, we can cultivate our ability to be present and mindful. We can learn to step back and become aware of our thoughts and emotions as they arise, and discern that they are just thoughts and emotions—they are not *me* and *mine*. We can become more open and adaptable. Instead of identifying totally with our hopes and fears, our ideas and thoughts, we can see that they are just empty phenomena which arise for a moment and then disappear.

We can be present. The ability to be present, to step back from our thoughts and see them as just thoughts, and our feelings as just feelings, allows us to become master of our mind instead of its slave. If you truly controlled things as you want, you would be able to say to yourself in the morning, "Okay, today I'm going to be happy, peaceful, well-adjusted, kind and compassionate and loving to everybody." And so it would be.

The first point in meditation, then, is to recognize that actually our minds are out of control. The Buddha described the average mind as like either a wild monkey or a drunken elephant in rut. If you've ever seen monkeys in the wild, you know that they spend their time eating, fighting, and copulating. As for elephants, during the mating season they are completely uncontrol-lable. And that is like the mind of most people: thinking about food; jumping around all over the place; stomping. This was the Buddha's assessment— before the advent of television—of the average mind!

The point is that we have a mind, a mind which we take with us every-where. We can go to the farthest reaches of the world, we can even go to the moon or to Mars, but we can never escape from our mind. Even when we sleep our mind is with us, active through our dreams. Our mind is con-stantly talking to us. It is our most intimate friend or enemy. Certainly, it is our most constant companion. But even so, generally, it is out of our control completely. And this is tragic.

We spend so much attention on matters of outer comfort and conve-nience, but even if you live in a palace, if your mind is out of control, you are miserable. You can live in a hovel, but if your mind is at peace, centered, you are happy. When I lived in the cave, I suppose outwardly it must have looked pretty bleak, but I was very happy. It was the happiest time of my life by far.

Once, I went to see my mother when she was living in Knightsbridge and working as the housekeeper for a very wealthy Canadian man. They were living in a very fancy part of London, and Hyde Park was just down the road. So there we were, in this very fancy apartment in the best part of London, with lots of wonderful food. There was everything you could possibly want, even two televisions. But I felt so bored really, and not very at ease in my own heart, which was my problem. And then I thought, "Well, please remember this whenever you think that external material comfort has anything what-ever to do with making the mind happy."

The point is that the state of our mind is where we dwell. And we really need to give much more attention to how we may cultivate a mind which is more peaceful, centered, and equanimous. Equanimous means that no matter what happens, we can cope with it. We don't have to manipulate everything to our own satisfaction.

At an interreligious conference some years ago, I met a Sufi singer from Turkey. He sang a very beautiful Sufi song about things that can go wrong in life, and the refrain rang out, "What of it?"

We traveled back to the New York airport together as we were both heading elsewhere. He was going back to Turkey. When we got to the airport, though, we discovered that none of his luggage had arrived. But he just grinned and shrugged and said, "What of it?"

And we all laughed! The whole situation was just a fact.

He said: "Oh, this is great. I don't have to take all that luggage anymore—I am free. I can just go."

I admired him tremendously because he was indeed taking his words onto the path. And so, when things go wrong, we can also say to ourselves, "What of it?"

People think that the Buddha was pessimistic because he spoke first about the unsatisfactoriness of our ordinary everyday existence. But he didn't leave it there. He didn't merely say, "Oh well, life is suffering; bad luck." He spoke of why it is suffering. Our everyday life is composed of suffering because we grasp. We hold on so tightly and yet everything is impermanent. Ultimately what we hold on to so tightly will change. It is not things which are the problem, it is our grasping mind.

We need to allow for meaning in our lives. That is, we need to get our own mind and life together. In this way, we can benefit the most people as well as ourselves. All the problems that really come in this world, apart from natural disasters, are caused by human beings. We cause endless problems with our out-of-control minds. Wisdom and compassion are desperately needed, and yet they dwell within our own minds. They can't be bought.

We need challenges in this world. And we have to cultivate qualities which in themselves cannot be cultivated unless we are faced with challenges. Far from being setbacks for our spiritual path, challenges are the spiritual path. We must develop an attitude which is open and which takes everything we meet and uses it. If things go wrong, if people are difficult, we cultivate patience and compassion. If people are in need, we cultivate generosity.

The Buddha said that to practice the Dharma is to be as a fish swimming upstream. Now, swimming upstream is a very lonely journey. You might ask yourself, Is it worth the time and effort to swim upstream when everybody else is going down with the current? But it is those who can swim upstream who reach the source. So if we want to do something meaningful with this lifetime, then the place to start is right where we are. And the only time to start is right now, in this moment. It is the only time we have. The future is just an idea. The past is gone. And the moment is flowing—like this.

The most valuable thing we have in our life is our mind. We can cultivate it. We can learn how to use our mind skillfully. At the moment this very precious jewel called a mind is covered with a thick casing of the mud of the eight worldly concerns, and we have to wash it clean so the jewel can sparkle again. We cannot say, "I don't have time," when every single breath we take, if we are conscious, is an expression of our practice.

☙ QUESTIONS

Q: My question is about how to deal with people who make you feel good. I think of my friends, because they make me feel good. They say these nice things about me and that's all right.

JTP: Well, that is all right, as long as you are happy and you also say nice things back to them and you love them. Ananda, the Buddha's assistant, once said that he'd been thinking about companionship, and he felt that it was half of the spiritual path. The Buddha said, "No, Ananda, good companionship is the whole of the spiritual path."

It is important to have good friends. But these good friends should be good friends because they also share good values—it doesn't mean that we just hang out with people who feed our ego. But if they also have good values, that means they encourage us toward the goodwill in ourselves. Then it is right and proper to appreciate and love them. The point is that the people who are not so nice to us and who pull us down and create problems for us are also worthy of our love and appreciation and goodwill. In this way we should not make so much distinction. Of course, naturally, you are going to like people who like you, and that's a bonus. But the important thing is to learn how to like people who don't like you. That's a practice.

Q: Sometimes people say very flattering things to me about how I am this or that, and it can make me feel uncomfortable. Sometimes it really seems over the top! And I'm not quite sure what to do in these sorts of situations. Do you have anything to suggest?

JTP: Well, you look at what they say! And you ask yourself, "Is this true?" Well, I mean I have a lot of people saying incredible things about me, and I look at them and I say to myself, "Well, really, is this true?" As far as I can see it is total rubbish. They know and I know it's not true. This is their very kind and gracious perception; it is their projection. You don't have to think that this means you actually have these qualities. If you do, well, that's very nice. But then you can also remember all the things which they are not mentioning which you have to work on. And likewise with criticism. If people criticize you, you can feel very grateful and look at them and say to yourself, "What they are saying about me, is that true? Have I not noticed that?" If it is true, I am very grateful they pointed this out because it is something I can work on. And if it is not true, then what's the problem? So either way, praise or blame, we can work on it.

Q: I have a question about something you said before—if we meet somebody, then we always look for praise. There might be occasions when this person doesn't appear to have goodwill and is harming people.

JTP: I didn't say you should praise them. I said that you should wish them well. Even if they are really horrible people, you should wish them happiness, and especially, the happiness of realizing their true nature. Genuine happiness. Because if they are connected with their true nature which is naturally happy, then they will change and they won't be horrible people. Maybe inside they have a lot of pain, even if they don't acknowledge it. People who are genuinely peaceful and happy and settled within themselves are usually not difficult to other people. And so therefore whoever you meet—you wish them well. It's not that you say, "Oh yeah, you're fantastic." Because maybe that person is not at all fantastic; maybe he or she is awful. But your compassion says, "May you be free from suffering; may you be happy." Your first feeling is a feeling of goodwill, whoever they are.

There is a story of Dudjom Rinpoche when he was in New York. Dudjom Rinpoche was the head of the Nyingma tradition. He was walking along a street, and somebody came up to him with a gun to mug him. Dudjom Rinpoche just looked straight into his eyes as he smiled at him, and bowed. The guy was so freaked out that he dropped his gun and ran! According to Dudjom Rinpoche's pure perception, he was just acknowledging the light within that person. Dudjom Rinpoche had no fear. And maybe he really transformed the man's life, who knows?

The point is that we should take everything that we meet in daily life and use it as the path; there is nothing to discard. We can't rest thinking only good things are worthy of practice while difficult things are obstacles to practice. Difficult things *are* the practice.

Q: Could you please explain what idiot compassion is?

JTP: This is an expression that comes from Chögyam Trungpa Rinpoche. I think he meant a kind of sentimental compassion. But really, it is very easy to be genuine. Compassion is conjoined with seeing clearly, and the more we see how things really are, the more we realize how messed up almost everybody is. You see the desperation in people's eyes because we are so locked in our ignorance. Even if somebody looks outwardly very affluent and happy and fine, we realize that they are still so vulnerable because they are acting from their ignorance and their ego-clinging: they are living far below their true potential, as almost everybody is. Acting like a little chicken—not understanding that we are all each truly a phoenix—is so sad.

We have this incredible potential as human beings—we have buddha nature—but look what we do with it. This is the underlying truth of compassion—it is when we realize the enormity of our dilemma, and how so few people are really sincerely interested in finding a way out. Even when they think they are. They may want to find a way out, but there are so many other things happening. Maybe tomorrow, they say. Opening to this underlying truth is to open to true compassion, and this is not mere pity or idiot compassion.

In England in the early 1960s, I became a Tibetan Buddhist of the Kagyu tradition. And so I was very happy to meet Chögyam Trungpa Rinpoche, a Kagyu lama. He came to England with Akong Rinpoche. Trungpa Rinpoche was going to study at Oxford University, but when he first arrived he stayed with a middle-class family. They invited me and my mother to go and meet him, which we did. In those days, of course, there were very few people interested in Tibetan Buddhism. This was in an era when mostly Theravadin Buddhism was practiced, and Zen and Tibetan Buddhism were looked on with suspicion. Trungpa Rinpoche didn't have many friends. The two Kagyu lamas arrived and they were put in Oxford and then what—there was John Driver, who was a Tibetan scholar who was there to help them, but they had very few friends. As a result, one weekend they would come to visit us in London and at the next weekend my mother and I would go to Oxford. In this way we got to know them quite well.

Trungpa Rinpoche was very interesting because he was nothing like what I imagined a lama should be. And yet I felt he was the real thing. I didn't know quite why, but I had met several lamas by this time, and I felt that somehow he had a certain quality which the others did not have.

And then Trungpa Rinpoche said to me one day, "Well, look. You might not believe this, but actually in Tibet I was quite a high lama and I never thought it would come to this. But please, can I teach you meditation? I must have *one* student!"

So I said, "Okay, if you feel like this."

None of us imagined that he would go on to have such an incredible influence on introducing Tibetan Buddhism to the West, and with such brilliance. Because in those days, his English was very limited; he struggled to express concepts beyond the range of his language. But he ended up with a facility in English that was so brilliant and innovative. He used the language to convey what he needed to express.

Tibetan lamas are educated to be extremely traditional. What is emphasized in their training is memorization and the ability to reproduce the words of former masters eloquently. Your own thoughts are not really appreciated unless they mirror the thoughts of the lineage lamas. Innovation is not appreciated on the whole. It's fascinating to see how many of the younger Tibetan lamas have taken their understanding of the Dharma and interpreted it anew for the very different minds which they meet in the West. I think it shows their sheer brilliance and the depth of their genuine understanding of the Dharma. They are offering their own genuine realization through extraordinary words which have no equivalent in Tibetan. And of course Trungpa Rinpoche led the way.

It is also interesting to see what happens when some of these lamas who are very innovative in English go back to speaking in Tibetan. Many of the younger Tibetans like to listen to English-language teachings—they can actually relate to them much more than to the more traditional Tibetan ways of expressing Dharma.

When lamas come to the West, where ceremonies are at a minimum, they are able to express whole other levels of their personality which normally wouldn't come out of them in a more traditional framework. Trungpa Rinpoche showed this very much. Because he had the karma to go to the West, a whole different expression of Dharma was given birth. It is pretty amazing what one person can do.

Q: There is this constant feeling of wanting to make an effort and yet still not really making enough effort. It is very difficult to really have enough compassion for myself, too.

JTP: Oh, absolutely. I think it is very important that we start where we are. When the Buddha taught loving-kindness and compassion—which we radiate to our loved ones and to people toward whom we feel fairly neutral and to those with whom we have problems and difficulties—he always emphasized that we have to start by giving compassion to ourselves. Ultimately, of course, we have to go beyond the ego and realize the nature of the mind. But in the meantime, in order to help us on the path, until we are at that state of pure awareness, we need to have an ego which is cooperating. We need a cooperating ego. Therefore we need to have a sense of self-esteem before we start breaking down the ego.

Shantideva, a great seventh-century Indian pandit, says that there is a huge distinction between pride and arrogance, which is a negative emotion, and self-confidence, which is essential on the path. The Tibetans translated the word *bodhisattva*, one who strives to obtain enlightenment out of compassion for all beings, as meaning an enlightened spiritual hero. We have to believe in ourselves, and in our own potential; we have to cooperate with ourselves, and encourage ourselves, and not be an obstacle on our own path.

So in the beginning we need to have an ego which is well adjusted, an ego which isn't always undermining our efforts. We don't diminish ourselves—that's not the point. That just creates a wounded, unhappy, desperate ego. It is an expression of ego when we're always pulling ourselves down, deprecating ourselves—thinking only about the worst in ourselves, and never encouraging ourselves by thinking of the good within us, our enormous potential for goodness.

We have to realize that this is the time. We don't know where we will be in our next life. This is our opportunity, now. And we can do it. So please—all of you—give a lot of time and attention to how to take your daily life and use it as your path. So that at the end, when you come to die, you can look back and think, "Well, this has been a life worth living." Maybe you are not radiating lights from a lotus twenty feet above the ground! But you have made some progress with this life. And that is something of benefit to you and to others.

There is a story of Drukpa Kunley, who was a great master, a yogi in the Drukpa Kagyu lineage. He went to Lhasa, to the Jowo Rinpoche statue, which is the most sacred statue in Tibet. It represents Shakyamuni Buddha.

Drukpa Kunley was very moved. He bowed down to the Buddha image and said, "You and I started out at the same time, but you attained enlightenment and I am still here in samsara. What is the difference between us? The difference between us is that you made the effort, and I am lazy."

And that goes for all of us. Why are we still stuck in samsara after all these lifetimes? Because we make excuses. Because we don't make the effort in the right direction. Patience and perseverance is the name of the game.

↜ 5

Renunciation

Renunciation, in Tibetan, is *nge jung*. *Nge jung* expresses the sense of definitely leaving a place. It means to get out. "Renunciation" does not have the same connotation in Tibetan as it does in English, in which there may be pain attached. In English, for example, you would say, he renounced his fatherland; he renounced his wealth; he renounced his patronage. There is always a sense here of giving up, but with a kind of pulling up and out by the roots. In other words, "renunciation" gives the sense of regretfully turning one's back on something which is desirable. Therefore, in Buddhist circles, when someone says, "You have to renounce something," everybody makes a face and says, "Uggh!"

The Tibetan sense of "renunciation" is a little different. For example, if you were to tell your children that they have to give up playing with their toys, they would find it very painful. But as children grow up they lose their fascination for these toys. They outgrow them. Leaving their toys behind does not seem like "renunciation" to them; it's just a matter of growing up. Likewise, in the spring and summer when the trees are full of leaves, there is resistance if we try to pull a leaf from a branch. But when autumn comes, the leaves spontaneously and of themselves part from the tree. Renunciation is closely aligned with this sense of parting. Outwardly it may seem like one is giving up something, and there might even be pain, but inwardly, interest in these things has been outgrown. Things fall away naturally.

In the 1960s and '70s there were Westerners who left for India to look for "spiritual truths." And on that journey there were those who came from affluent and well-endowed families. They had a lot to give up. They slept in dirty hotels, ate quite inedible food, and with joy, because they were getting so much more in return. It did not seem to them that what they were giving up was of value.

When the Lord Buddha left his palace and all his wealth and family, there was not a twinge of regret. I am sure the only thing he did feel was a pang in his heart for the welfare of his wife and young son. But he was going toward spiritual liberation, which is so much vaster, so much greater than anything he was leaving behind. Even the loss of his small son paled before all that there was to gain, and not just for himself, but for all beings. Some feminists get quite upset with the Buddha for having left behind his wife and small son, but had he not renounced his princely life, then for a start, we would not be inquiring into the nature of our lives in this way.

In our life we have to set values. What really matters to us in this life? If we don't ask ourselves such questions, we just meander; we just try to keep comfortable. In order to have a definite direction, we need to set a purpose for ourselves. We need to ask ourselves, What would be a life well lived? Once we have set our purpose, we have to work out what things lead us along on that path and what things are merely distractions.

Many people ask how enlightenment can be achieved. And a few, very few, ask how they may develop genuine renunciation. Such questions are like asking how one may grow a bodhi tree in one's heart. Now in order to grow a bodhi tree properly, we need first to prepare the ground. We have a plot of land, and that is called our heart, our heart center. As with any other plot of ground in which you are trying to grow a plant, first you have to pro-tect it.

We may protect the ground of our heart through the observance of five basic ethical principles, or precepts. I am sure that the majority of us know these basic principles of living in this world harmlessly—not taking life, not taking what has not been given, not lying, not engaging in sexual misconduct, and not taking intoxicants. Not taking life includes not only human beings, but animals, fish, and insects; not taking anything that has not been given to us includes returning anything that we have borrowed, such as books, DVDs, and so forth. The precept on sexual misconduct means being responsible for one's sexual conduct—not using any person in any exploitative way, not engaging in any kind of sexual relationship which could cause any possible harm to anybody at any point in time. The precept on intoxicants arises because they usually affect the mind. When people are under the influence of alcohol and drugs, they can become violent and abusive. Compassion and the loving aspects of our nature are ignored. After all, Buddhism deals with the mind—how one may become its master rather than its slave.

Let us look at the precept about speech, because we are very affected by the speech of others. It is not just the words we say but the tone in which we say them. Often when there are fights and disagreements people part from one another because of words. Standing back from oneself and just listening as one speaks—not judging, but just listening as though one were outside oneself—is a very skillful practice. Our words are a very important part of our conduct. Which means our words should be truthful. And they should be kind and non-divisive. Our words should not set one person against another. There is no need to indulge in meaningless talk and gossip; there is no need to create hurt and disharmony. We have this wonderful gift of language; let us treasure it and be responsible for spreading harmony and happiness among all people, especially our colleagues and our family. These precepts are not commandments. They are a form of training we undertake to help us naturally bring our conduct and speech into conformity with that of an enlightened being.

So now we have made a fence around our garden. But we must also consider the ground itself. In general, this ground has hardly been worked for many years. It is full of good and bad habits, and it is full of judgments and prejudices which have never been queried. It is full of absorption in *me*, and full of things that are *mine*. And the ground is full of memories that we have never seriously sorted through.

When you want to travel lightly, carrying everything on your back, you sort through all your things. You have to decide what is essential and what is not essential. You have to make clear choices. And so it is with all the clutter and junk that sits in the mind.

In traditional texts, the idea of renunciation, of *nge jung*, is closely associated with the idea of leaving one's homeland, because these ideals are based on the traditional Buddhist view that we should go from home life to the homeless life and henceforth wander. If you read traditional texts, like *The Words of My Perfect Teacher* by Patrul Rinpoche, you know that it is regarded as a sine qua non of the spiritual life that the first thing you do is leave your home and wander off. You leave behind home, family, friends, possessions, and so forth, and away you go. Naturally, many people, not least Tibetans, read that and ignore it! The most they manage is to move in to the local monastery and arrange for support by their family. But foreigners when they read these books take such views very seriously and become quite alarmed. Because they have no intention of leaving behind their family, friends, and country, they feel that they have failed before they even started. But it is not things or people which are the problem—it is our attachment to things and people.

The point is not so much outer renunciation, leaving home and family; what we need to work on is inner renunciation. Genuine renunciation comes when we outgrow our fascination with and involvement in worldly things— when we outgrow what had once seemed so important to us.

When I first became Buddhist, I was in London in the early 1960s. I didn't know any other Buddhists. I read a text that said we had to renounce the world, and I thought, "Right." I was eighteen years old. Promptly I packed up all my clothes, handed them to my mother and said, "You give them away."

As I did not know what Buddhist renunciants looked like, I got this dress made, which had a hole for my head to go through and two holes for my arms and was just gathered around the waist. It was a bit like a Greek tunic. I wore flat shoes, pulled my hair back, and wore no makeup. I went round like this for several months. Eventually I discovered that there was a Buddhist society in London, and so my mother and I went to visit. The Buddhist society in London was full of middle-aged, middle-class ladies, none of whom was wearing a Greek tunic. But they were wearing high heels and makeup! Since I assumed they were more experienced than me, I thought maybe I had made a bit of a mistake somewhere!

"What a pity I gave away all my clothes!" I said to my mother. My very wise mother handed me the key to her wardrobe, and inside it I found all my clothes.

I had never been anywhere in my life until I first went to India in 1964. In those days, you did not really have backpacks. You had bags made of canvas or leather that you carried by the handles, which made them very heavy. I knew that where I was going, Dalhousie, was up in the mountains, which meant I would face cold weather. I also knew that India was hot. So I tried to pack for both. After folding my two long thick nightgowns made of warm flannel, I reached for my two pretty gingham ones that also went all the way to the ground. Before I left, someone gave me two very pretty little nylon nightgowns, and so I took those, too. In one bag I had six nightgowns.

Disorganized, in total disarray, the garden of our mind contains some very precious plants, but mostly it is all overladen with junk. And so we have three choices: we could live in the garbage dump, and leave it at that. Or we could say, "Aha! Garbage dump," and begin to pull out the pieces of garbage one by one, looking at each piece: "Oh, that is interesting!" But of course this takes a long time, and in fact, since the amount of garbage we have been accumulating is endless, it will take us an endless amount of time to throw it all out, especially as more keeps coming in! Our third option is to recognize our garbage as mulch, as compost, and in this way feed the precious plants.

In our nunnery we have a lot of vegetable peelings and tea leaves and other material which we need to throw away. The only sensible thing to do with it is to create a compost heap. Initially, when the nunnery was founded, the girls just threw it outside, and it ended up as a great big smelly disgusting hill. So we invited an expert to teach them how to make compost properly. The essential points consist of aerating it and putting in little worms, but I won't go into detail here. It makes a good analogy, though, to dealing with the rubbish in our minds. Because if we just leave it there, building up and accumulating, we end up living in the middle of a garbage heap, within which we try to make a little space for ourselves to feel at home. And of course our society does not help at all, because practically everything it contributes is just more garbage. So the point is, instead of allowing all of it to become just this solid, compact load of junk, we need to aerate it. If it can be aerated through pure awareness, then of itself, without any effort from our side, the garbage turns into this very friable and highly fertile compost which can then be used to grow our bodhi tree.

People think if something is very difficult or complicated it must be good, but often it is the simplest things which are best. But because something is so simple, we don't believe it. Truly, even our most advanced yogis say that their practice is really very, very simple.

All true spiritual paths deal with how to dissolve this small sense of self to open to something which is so much vaster, whatever we may call that. For example, St. Paul said, "It is not I who moves and speaks, but Christ who moves in me." But in the meantime, ironically, we also need—while we are living in our relative world, in our conceptual mind—to become friends with this sense of ego as an aid on our journey. Ultimately, the ego does not exist. At least, it does not exist in the way we see it. But in the meantime, when we say we have to overcome the ego, this does not mean that we can overcome it by beating it to death.

In the beginning, as we embark on our inner journey, we need to become at ease with ourselves, gain confidence in ourselves, and in this way, slowly, we can see through the duplicity of our minds. One of the most important aspects of the Buddhist path is the cultivation of the mind called meditation. The following is a simple but effective method suitable for most practitioners.

Meditation

There are three parts to meditation, and they are easy. They are simple.

Step one

Whether you are sitting on a cushion or in a chair, sit up straight. The important thing is to keep your back straight and your feet flat on the floor. Bring your shoulders up; bring them backwards and down again, and that way you are in a good posture. Now just relax. Otherwise, you will get tired.

Focus your attention on the coming and going of the breath. The breath is a good focus for practice because there is a strong connection between our breath and our state of mind. Be aware of your breath as it comes and goes. With the breath as a focus, you are present. You cannot breathe in the past or in the future. You can only breathe now. Normally, we are not conscious of our breathing. But the moment we are conscious of it, we bring our mind into the present. This is skillful means. You can become conscious of your breath during the day, at any time: driving, walking, sitting at your computer, even while you are talking. Breathing in; breathing out. And that in itself is a meditation. Even sitting up straight, holding a formal pose, is not required for this.

According to the Tibetan tradition, one should be able to keep the mind one-pointedly on twenty-one breaths without being distracted. Thoughts are no problem. Following after and identifying with thoughts is the problem. Thoughts can be like a river, with us right in the middle getting tossed up and down. Becoming conscious of our thoughts is a way to step out of that river. As you step out of the current of the river you can focus your attention on what is forefront: your breath, as it rises and falls, especially your outgoing breath. You may count *one*, as you breathe in; *two*, as you breathe out. Don't give the thoughts in the back of the mind any attention. If by any chance you jump back into the river and get swept along, climb out onto the bank, and start again.

One, as you breathe in; *two*, as you breathe out. Keeping the mind very relaxed, centered, you just concentrate on the breath as it comes in and as it goes out. And that is all you have to do. Nothing else in the world matters right now, except to breathe in and out and to know it.

Step two

Now take that spotlight of awareness that is centered on the breath, and turn it inward to the thoughts themselves. Our thoughts are constantly flowing by, moment to moment to moment. The contents of the river are ever-changing. But now, as we're very relaxed, we can step out from the river and rest on the bank. We can just watch the river go past without immersing ourselves.

We are not judging our thoughts at this time. We are not thinking that this is a clever thought, or a terrible or stupid or interesting thought; they are just thoughts. Whatever thoughts arise inside of us, whatever sounds arise outside of us, all are just thoughts, just sounds, and are not important. What is important is the knowing quality, the knowing quality that is centered on the flow of thoughts. Normally, when we are thinking, we *are* the thoughts. But now we are stepping back and becoming a witness to the thoughts, an observer. So there is the thought current and there is that which is aware of the thought current.

Keep the mind very relaxed but very centered; you're just seeing the thoughts as they flow by and not becoming involved with them. Try that for five minutes and see how you get on.

Whatever sounds you hear are just sounds and are not important. Don't follow them. Whatever thoughts you have in your mind are just thoughts. Don't get fascinated by the thoughts; don't follow them. Just keep sitting on the bank. See if you can make as it were a separation in the mind between the flow of thoughts and the awareness that knows.

Step three

The third step is the easiest step of all. You just rest in that awareness. Now you might think you don't have any awareness, but the very fact that you can think and know that you are thinking is a manifestation of awareness. Normally, though, we are not conscious of being conscious. Just sit and be aware of being aware. There is absolutely nothing to do.

We always want to be doing something, and this is the problem. We always think, "What do I do?" This is one of the reasons why other aspects of

Tibetan meditation such as visualization of deities and mantra recitation are so popular: there is so much to do. But it can leave you going, "Huh?" You can see the mind running around, looking for something to hold on to. But I am describing the kind of meditation in which we just sit. We just sit to sit. It is very akin to Soto Zen. We just sit, without thinking about it. We are just conscious of being here.

There is nothing to do; there is nothing to concentrate on; there is nothing else but to be in this moment, as it is. Technically speaking, if you want an official name for this kind of meditation, it is called "resting in the nature of mind."

All you have to do is do nothing. Just sit here, and be aware of just sitting. Usually, what happens is that we become more conscious of energies flowing through the body, a sense of being. But don't try to manufacture anything, just be very open to whatever happens.

The quickest way to stop suffering is to recognize our lack of identification with our thoughts and feelings. Normally, we try to get beyond our underlying dissatisfaction by distracting ourselves. We try to lift up our sense of ego by feeding it with as much pleasure as possible. We distract ourselves endlessly, so we don't have to see that underneath it all is deep dissatisfaction. For example, it is noticeable in the United States, which has such a high level of material prosperity, that practically everyone who can afford it seems to have their own private therapist or psychiatrist, just as they have their own dentist or doctor. So clearly, even having so much pleasure and comfort in one's life does not actually cover up the underlying dis-ease, or what the Buddha called *dukkha*.

Actually, "dis-ease" is a good translation for *dukkha*, which is the opposite of *sukha*, meaning ease, the seemingly smooth and nice. As we come to recognize dukkha, dis-ease, within ourselves, we come to recognize just how sick we are with the three poisons of desire, hatred, and confusion. Renunciation is a matter of letting go. And the ultimate renunciation is to release one's grasp at a self-autonomous, enduring, and separate *me* at the center of the universe.

One of the fastest ways to gain realization is through really observing the mind—observing the thoughts and seeing that we are not our thoughts. Thoughts rise and thoughts fall. But we are not the thoughts. There is something *behind* the thoughts: there is a consciousness, an awareness, behind the coming and going of thoughts. And that is what we have to pay more attention to, especially during practice. Our mind is like a clever computer. We can program it very well, but that is not the energy driving the computer. We have to reconnect with the energy behind the computer, and meditation is a way to bring us back to that. The energy source is vast. Our computer is just one little computer, but this energy is vast and all-encompassing.

The problem is that most people feel cozy enough in samsara. They do not really have the genuine aspiration to go beyond samsara; they just want samsara to be a little bit better. It is quite interesting that "samsara" became the name of a perfume. And it is like that. It seduces us into thinking that it is okay: samsara is not so bad; it smells nice! The underlying motivation to go beyond samsara is very rare, even for people who go to Dharma centers. There are many people who learn to meditate and so forth, but with the underlying motive that they hope to make themselves feel better. And if it ends up making them feel worse, instead of realizing that this may be a good sign, they think there is something wrong with Dharma. We are always looking to make ourselves comfortable in the prison house. We might think that if we get the cell wall painted a pretty shade of pale green, and put in a few pictures, it won't be a prison any more.

Traditionally, renunciation is combined with the purification of spiritual motivation known as bodhichitta. *Bodhi* basically means enlightenment, and *chitta* means heart or mind. So *bodhichitta* means the thought or the aspiration of enlightenment. There are two basic reasons we follow a spiritual path and look for liberation. One reason is that we want to be free. Let's take the traditional example of a burning house: your whole house is on fire, and you run out from it. But all your family—your partner, your children, your parents, even your pet dog—are all still inside. What are you going to do? You don't just say, "Well, I'm out. So too bad. Do your best to get out, too." Naturally this leads to the second basic reason for following a spiritual path: we will try to pull them out as well.

Let's take another example: suppose there is a huge swamp, and we are all drowning in it. Somehow, through tremendous effort, you manage to pull yourself out onto dry land. What are you going to do? Do you turn to face your family and your friends, do you turn to everyone still drowning in the swamp, and say, "Well folks, sorry. I am free on dry land, and if you really struggle hard, you can get out too—bye!" Even in a worldly situation, if one were on dry land, one would use that position to try to pull the others out.

Likewise, on the spiritual path, it is understood that to aspire for merely one's own spiritual well-being and freedom is actually inherently selfish. In this light we may find that the only real reason to strive spiritually for ever-deepening wisdom and compassion is our wish to help others likewise gain liberation. This aspiration, this complete turnaround in our whole motivation for striving on the spiritual path, is called bodhichitta.

Often people who regard themselves as being on a so-called spiritual path tend to become rather self-preoccupied: my practice, my guru, my path, my experiences, my realizations. While the spiritual path is intended to lead us to decrease and eventually to abandon completely our obsession with the ego, very often people use it to inflate the ego. They become very ambitious. Spiritual practice becomes for them just another form of achievement. Now, it is not just a matter of getting a promotion at your firm, or earning more money, or getting a bigger car or a bigger house. It is also a matter of which high lamas you meet; how many super-secret initiations you receive that nobody else ever receives; all the special inner instructions and realizations which you have obtained; how long your own retreat was, compared with that of others; and how your own retreat site was located in a yet more remote place. Bodhichitta counteracts all that, because we are now practicing not for ourselves but for others.

Becoming a bodhisattva, a spiritual hero, is not somehow a quick fix. The bodhisattva vow is a total commitment, through all one's lives, in whatever form, to be here for the benefit of others until samsara is emptied. And when we become very high-level bodhisattvas, at the very last minute we may hear, "No, after you." "No, no—you first!" "No, I have a vow! You first!"

But until that time we all hold hands and jump together. The point is that the bodhisattva vow is a complete change in motivation and attitude. One doesn't have to underline it and say whether it is possible or not possible. The point is that it completely turns around one's whole motivation for traveling the path. As the *Diamond Sutra* points out, ultimately there are no sentient beings to be saved, since the idea of a sentient being as a separate being is the delusion we are seeking to overcome in order to be enlightened.

What keeps us in samsara is our belief in ourselves as individual sentient beings. Therefore, the vow to save everybody already contains two wrong views: the belief in an "I" that will save sentient beings, and the belief that there are sentient beings to be saved. Nonetheless, although there is no one to save them and nothing to be saved, one still takes the vow to save all beings. Bodhichitta manifests on two levels: there is ultimate bodhichitta and relative bodhichitta. Ultimate bodhichitta understands the non-inherent existence of all beings, called emptiness. But it also understands the interconnection of all phenomena, or the interdependence of all beings. So on an ultimate level, there is nothing to be saved, because we are already enlightened. But on a relative level, which is where most of us live, it definitely looks as if there are sentient beings who are caught in the swamp of samsara and need to be pulled out.

Wisdom says there is nothing to be done; it has already happened. But compassion says, "Get to work! Start pulling!" These two aspects unfold together: the wisdom aspect, which sees that ultimately there is nothing to be done; and the relative aspect, which says, nonetheless, we have a lot of work to do. But of course we cannot start pulling all these endless beings out of the swamp if we are still drowning in the swamp ourselves. To use an analogy, suppose we want to be doctors. First of all, we have to go to medical school for many years to study how to use medicine properly. You might say, "No, no, no. I can't waste that time; that would be really selfish. I have to go and help these poor people; they are sick, and they need me!" You might grab a bag full of medicine, and a scalpel, and rush off to help. There is a lot of compassion in that, but it lacks wisdom, as you might give the wrong medicine to people, and heaven knows what you might do with the scalpel! Intention is good, but the point is that such actions may do more harm than good because one lacks skillful means. Whereas if one has patience and goes to medical school, studies hard, and practices under skilled teachers, one can find an infinite number of people out there to help. Milarepa was a great Tibetan yogi of the eleventh century. One of his students said, "Look here, all these people are suffering. It is very selfish for us just to go away and meditate. We should be out helping people." Milarepa replied:

> For as long as sky and space exist, there will be sentient beings
>   for us to help.

But in order to help you must first be able to help, and that comes through practice and study. From a Buddhist point of view, as we come back again and again, any knowledge, and especially any understanding or realization that we gain in one lifetime, will be carried over into the next life. This is why meditation and study come very easily for some and not for others.

Bodhichitta should underlie everything that we do. Our life on this planet is not merely for our own sake, our own comfort and enjoyment. Our life is not even just for the sake of our own spiritual progress. We are here to learn and practice and to get into a position to help others learn and practice.

Inherently we are all buddhas. We are completely perfect. We just have to learn how to recognize our true, absolutely immaculate, wise, and compassionate nature. We are not looking to take something from outside ourselves. Renunciation really is just a matter of letting go. We are opening up to what we already have—we are opening up to the fullness within us. We are trying simply to awaken to our original nature.

✎ Questions

Q: Can you speak of the four kinds of right effort in relation to cultivating our garden? We uproot negative emotions; we don't let them come up again; we cultivate the good. What is the fourth right effort?

JTP: The fourth right effort is about encouraging the future good plants to come. You uproot all the weeds, and you stop future weeds. Likewise, you take care of the good plants that are there, and you encourage future good plants to arise. It is very important, as we come to recognize our faults and take measures to deal with them, that we also appreciate the goodness in ourselves—the good things, the things which are going right, and to *encourage* those, because if we don't encourage the good, then like a plant with no sunlight or water, the goodness just grows spindly.

In all schools of Buddhism, after regretting and feeling remorse for the wrong that we have done, we should also rejoice and encourage ourselves in all the good that we have done, not in order to become proud but in order to restore a kind of balance within ourselves. If we only zero in on all the wrong within us, then that undercuts our own self-esteem, our own confidence, and our own appreciation that we also have good qualities. If we lived always with a companion who was endlessly pointing out our faults but never ever encouraged us to notice the good things, then that would be a very unpleasant sort of companion. A good companion, of course, from time to time, points out our faults so that we can correct them. But they also give us some compliments, too, to encourage us to do better. In Buddhism it is not regarded as a virtue to see oneself constantly as a poor, helpless sinner. We are bodhisattvas on the path, with the potential for enlightenment glowing within us.

Q: Jetsunma, I have a question related to your nunnery. In the documentary film *Cave in the Snow* and in the slide presentation, the *togdenma* tradition was mentioned. Could you tell us a little bit more about that?

JTP: In our monastery at Tashi Jong, called Khampagar, they have a tradition which they brought from Tibet, of what are called *togdens*, or realized ones. They are monks who go into long-term retreat to practice especially the Six Yogas of Naropa. They are taken out of the monastery and disappear. The image which I use is that of making bread. First you have the dough, which you put in a hot oven. You close the oven door, and then you leave the dough in there until it is completely cooked, because if you take it out when it is half-baked, then it will just collapse, and will be unpalatable. But if you leave the dough in the oven until it is completely cooked all the way through, then when you take it out as bread, it does not collapse, and is both delicious and nourishing. So these yogis, when they are finally released, so to say, and are seen again, they not only have actual realizations but their realizations are stabilized.

My lama, the previous Khamtrul Rinpoche, at one time said to me there were also females of this lineage in Tibet, but due to the events there, that lineage was broken; and he always prayed that I would re-establish this very precious female lineage. So I went to Amdo in Tibet to meet the head of the Drukpa lineage who was a very old lama called Adeu Rinpoche, to request him to give this transmission to some of our nuns. He knew about this, and he agreed to do so, although he said it would take six months to give the transmission. Unfortunately the next year he died. So now we are trying to get the transmission through the present Khamtrul Rinpoche. There are problems, but eventually it will happen. It has to do with the fact that the female and male lineages are slightly different. But in the meantime, we do have five nuns who are in a three-year retreat, and they are being taught by our most senior togden. At least we have started.

Q: The second part of my question relates to the bhikshuni ordination. I have just read in a German magazine that Venerable Thubten Chodron in the United States has started to give full ordination, and I wonder what the situation is in your nunnery. How do you deal with the subject?

JTP: As to the bhikshuni lineage, at the moment this is not happening in the Tibetan tradition. The main problem is that there is a lot of opposition from the monks. So without the sense of consensus from the monastic order, the higher lamas don't want to go forward. I should explain to those who do not know what we are talking about: in Tibet, nuns can only receive the novice ordination; they cannot receive the full ordination. However, many nuns have been studying now for fifteen, eighteen, twenty years. And they have not received any kind of official recognition or degree. Some of the nuns now want to become geshes and khenmos, and they really hope for this. His Holiness the Dalai Lama said, "Yes, it is right: you should get this." But in a recent meeting in Dharamsala, certain lamas, geshes, said of the nuns, "No, they can never become geshes because they are not fully ordained, and since they are not fully ordained, they cannot become geshes." So that is it. Because the nuns are not fully ordained, they cannot study the monastic code and be examined on it.

So I am hoping because of this total rejection the nuns will now say, "We want to be geshes. We have studied for eighteen years; we have a right. And if it means we have to have full ordination, then we are going for it." If they push, then something might happen.

Q: You said renunciation is difficult to attain, but monastics already have some renunciation when they take their vows. It seems a bit of a contradiction to me.

JTP: All these qualities which are praised are simply ways for us to aspire. Of course renunciation is difficult, but we can renounce. Of course bodhichitta is difficult, but we can develop it. If it were impossible, spiritual masters would not tell us to do it.

Q: You said it was difficult for lay people and for monastics to develop renunciation?

JTP: Of course renunciation is easier if you are renounced, and that is why the Buddha started the sangha. But it does not mean that as lay people you cannot also practice contentment through having fewer possessions. Practicing the joy of giving and of sharing is also a form of renunciation. And the ultimate renunciation is the renunciation of our self-concern, our self-grasping mind. In this, monks and nuns are in as bad trouble as lay people, I assure you.

Q: My question relates to your teaching about anger. I have experienced a difficult situation of anger arising. I felt the anger, but somehow I could not step back far enough to let it go. Do you have a certain technique, or what advice would you give in this way?

JTP: Of course anger is something that comes up again and again in people's lives, and so there are a number of techniques. But as with every technique, it does not always work the first time. You have to practice. The best method, and one which Longchen Rabjam would definitely approve of, is that at the moment of anger arising—at the very moment it arises—if we recognize it, then the anger transforms of itself into a very powerful wisdom energy. This is a very tricky thing, though, because normally by the time we have discovered that we are angry, the anger is already quite developed. We didn't see it at the first bare moment.

Of course the traditional way to work with anger is to recognize that our anger is also—and really this is an important thing to remember—our opportunity to develop patience. Anybody who has a problem with anger definitely should read the chapter on patience in Shantideva's *Bodhicharyavatara* (*The Way of the Bodhisattva*). If we don't have anybody, or any situation, which upsets us, we can never learn how to deal skillfully with our anger. Forbearance and patience are very important qualities to develop. Therefore, instead of resenting and getting angry with someone who annoys us, we should feel gratitude because this is our opportunity to start putting all these ideas into actual practice. These ideas of the Dharma are very wonderful, but if they just stay up in the head, they are not going to help at all. So we really have to look at what our weaknesses are. As I say again and again, it is like going to a gymnasium. At a gymnasium, a trainer will look at you and immediately point out your weak parts. And those are the bits he will get you to work on. So therefore, a particular weak spot where, for example, we get angry easily, or jealous, or greedy—that is our opportunity. That is our good fortune. We can really make a difference by dealing with the problem and turning it around.

That is why our biggest challenges are our greatest opportunities. In addition, if you have somebody or something habitually pressing your buttons, then when you are sitting in meditation and you are nice and calm, you can replay the situation again. And while you are quiet you can really see how it was, and then you can rewrite the script. Where did it start to go wrong?

One needs to do that again and again. You do see a certain pattern, and what we need to do is to start reworking the pattern. As one's awareness becomes stronger, when anger arises, one recognizes it—*I am angry*. And one accepts that. And then one lets it go. It takes work, but it can happen.

One of the most beautiful togdens in our monastery, whom everybody loved—he was so completely loving, his eyes just beamed with love—had once been a monk who was so angry and so nasty that the other monks finally said to him, "You know, either you train to be a togden or you leave the monastery." So then he really worked on his mind. He really practiced a lot of lojong, mind-training; he really worked hard on compassion, and in the end he became the most loving being.

We can change. It is very important to realize that our biggest flaw is our greatest opportunity to transform.

Q: Is there a kind of destiny or calling for us humans? One practices Dharma, and there is the feeling of being destined to do something. The second part of my question is about the power of positive thoughts. How strong is the power of positive thought, and is it a form of attachment?

JTP: As to the idea of a calling, of course from a Buddhist point of view, that would be the result of very strong imprints from past lives. For example, if someone had in many lifetimes been a musician, then probably he would in this lifetime have a calling toward music; or if someone had spent many lives on a spiritual path, then they would in this life again be drawn to spiritual teachings from an early age.

As to positive and negative thinking, certainly it has now been proved that if we have very negative emotions in our mind, such thinking affects every cell in our body. So it is very likely, if negative thinking does not make us actually ill, that it certainly does not help in our healing process. Likewise, positive emotions and positive thoughts have a positive effect on the cells of our body and could help in a healing process.

We are all inwardly very interconnected. Every cell of our body has an intelligence. And our thoughts and feelings have very strong repercussions outside our brains. Clearly on a very practical level, even if we are very sick, to dwell in positive thoughts is much nicer than to dwell in negative thoughts. Positive thoughts bring happiness, and negative thoughts bring suffering. Even though the body may be suffering, there is no reason for the mind to suffer. Sending positive thoughts throughout one's body and out into the universe seems to me like good common sense. I don't see why it is attachment. I think right now the world is in great need of positive good thinking.

Q: I know many women with low self-esteem. Why is that?

JTP: I would say that buddha nature is neither male nor female; that the perfection of wisdom, Prajnaparamita, is female; and that with the opportunities for education which we now have, there is nothing in this life that cannot be attained in a female body. And what is more, women are naturally receptive to meditation. Many great meditation masters have told me, without my asking, that women are better at meditation. They are intellectually very well attuned, and now that we have the opportunities, there is nothing that we cannot do in a female body. So, go for it.

Male or female, we have intelligence. We have compassion locked away in our heart. Buddha nature has no gender. The Dharma is the same whether we are male or female, and the only thing we lack is the determination to start and to keep going. If we work at it there is nothing which any single one of us cannot attain. But we have to do it, and not just think about it. We have to work at it. If we don't work, then nothing changes. If we work, then everything changes.

✧ 6

The Six Perfections

THE PATH OF the six perfections, or paramitas, is the path of a
bodhisattva. And a bodhisattva is someone who aspires to attain
enlightenment to benefit not only themselves but also others. *Paramita* literally means something which goes beyond. *Param* means "beyond"; and *ita*
means "to travel." To go beyond. There is no actual English equivalent, but
usually the paramitas are translated as the six perfections: generosity, ethical
conduct, patience, enthusiastic effort, meditation, and wisdom. The path
of the six perfections is a complete path in many ways, because it incorpo-
rates qualities that are needed for a well-balanced spiritual life, a spiritual life
which is not only directed inwardly, through meditation and wisdom, but
also directed outwardly, through generosity, harmlessness, the development
of patience, and so on.

In a traditional Buddhist country, the main practitioners are usually monks
and nuns. Therefore the Dharma discourses are aimed at those who have
more or less devoted their lives to the practice of the spiritual path. Monastics usually have more time. Even if they live in a monastery where there
are many things to do, they still have far fewer distractions than those in
the household life. Monastics don't have a family life or close relationships;
they don't need to succeed in a career; they don't have an outside social life;
nor do they have television and other entertainments. The monastic life is
usually centered around a study program, meditation retreats, or the perfor-
mance of rituals.

However, nowadays in the West this situation is completely reversed. Most
Dharma audiences are made up of lay people. That means they probably are
in close relationships—they might be married, they might have children or

parents for whom they are responsible. They have professions and a social life. How much time is left over for study, meditation, and prayer? In this we find a profound difference between the lives of monastics and lay people.

If we present Buddhism as a path of meditation and formal practice— meaning the time when we go to the temple or to the Dharma center, the time when we are actually sitting in meditation, doing our rituals or what- ever—we might think of the rest of the day as so much a waste of time, a hin- drance to our practice. But as lay people, the amount of time we are able to give to formal practice is too small to effect a real radical change if for the rest of the day our mind is totally distracted. It is not enough if we use only half an hour or so a day trying to get our mind together. So we have to re-examine the whole situation. In order to really actualize an inner transformation, an inner change, we have to realize that everything we do, every encounter we have, every breath we take, if done with genuine awareness and understand- ing, is the practice of Dharma.

Far from being an obstacle to our practice, our relationships and careers when used skillfully *are* the practice. Merging or integrating our daily life and the spiritual path, we can realize that the two are one if done with sufficient awareness and appreciation. In order to explain this, I use the six paramitas as a kind of basic structure, because they include all levels of practice. We will deal first with generosity, and go on to discuss ethics, patience, and enthusias- tic effort or perseverance. Finally, we will come to meditation and wisdom.

Dana paramita, or generosity

The Buddha put *dana,* which means "giving," or "generosity," in Sanskrit, at the very beginning of the bodhisattva path because it is something we all can do. However deluded we may be, however angry we may be, however jealous or greedy we may be, we can still give. It is a very basic quality. We don't need to attain any spiritual heights to learn how to give. Giving means to open up the hands and heart. It is a very beautiful way to respond to others.

In Asia, people understand very well this whole quality of open-hearted giving and generosity. It is based on the understanding that if we want to be prosperous and successful not only now but in our future lives, we have to plant seeds. We are not going to get a harvest if we don't plant seeds. The seeds for prosperity are generosity and giving. Therefore, if we want to have success, we have to create the causes for that. If we have a hard time getting

money, if we are always ending up very poor, it is because we haven't created enough causes through open-heartedness and generosity in the past.
The Buddha said that if people understood the true future benefits of giving,
they would not keep even one meal to themselves. They would try to share
that meal, too. But because we don't see future results, we think, "If I give
something away, then what will I have? What will be left for me?" That kind
of mind not only cuts off our generous impulses, it also creates the causes for
not being prosperous later.

It is a joy to give! It is the closed-mindedness of "This is me; this is mine;
and I am not giving to anyone else" which causes us so much inner pain and
prevents us from really appreciating what we have. You see, it isn't the things
we own which are the problem; it's our clinging to them, our grasping, which
is the problem.

Do things own us, or do we own them? Are we able to hold things lightly,
so that when we see someone in need or just feel appreciation, we can give?
In India, I had a friend who was a Hindu swami, and he lived in a very simple
ashram not so far from our nunnery. He was actually a direct disciple of the
great Indian sage Ramana Maharshi who was from south India. Our friend
the swami had many disciples from all over India and from abroad. But he
lived very simply. People were always bringing him things that were rarely
seen, and so very appreciated, in India. And yet when anybody gave him
anything, no matter what it was, his first thought was, "Who would be a good
person for me to give this to?"

Nothing stuck to his fingers. Whatever he was holding would slide off into
somebody else's hands. And he was happy, because his life was one of con-
tinual receiving and handing over. There was no accumulation. There was
no having to carry his possessions and his fear of losing them as a heavy burden on his back. But all this is not to say that you should go home and clear
out all your things. Rather the point is opening the heart, really being able to
rejoice in giving to others, and not just material things. Material things are
good to start with, but we can also give our time and our sympathy. We can
be there for others when they need us. We can give our fearlessness.

In Buddhist parlance, there are three kinds of giving. First, there is the
giving of material gifts. Second, there is the gift of the Dharma. That means
being there for others, listening to them, trying to help them, even trying to
help them clarify their minds a little bit by giving advice. And then there
is also the gift of fearlessness, of being a means of protection, and helping

others to discover their own inner courage—to give that to someone is a priceless gift.

We can start to give in simple ways by developing this quality of being conscious of others and of their needs. We can give joy and pleasure through our intention to help others. Not giving only at Christmas or on birthdays or when we are visiting, but giving spontaneously—we see something we like, and we give it to somebody, maybe even to somebody we don't like. Giving to people whom we don't like is a beautiful way to relate to others. The Buddha stressed the importance of generosity—this quality of joy in giving to others and not always holding to the sense of "what can I get for me."

Traditionally, there are three different kinds of recipients of giving that are recommended for us. First, one can offer to those whom one regards in some way as worthy of gifts. That means, in Buddhist parlance, the buddhas and bodhisattvas. It means the monastic sangha; it means one's spiritual teacher or any teacher whom one regards as an inspiration and spiritual superior. We offer out of honor and respect.

The second group of recipients can include those to whom we give because of our gratitude, and that particularly means our parents. It also means our teachers, and anyone who has helped us in any way. We are grateful. This quality of honoring, of gratitude and respect, has become so denigrated in our present world, and it is one of the reasons why our society is disintegrating. We don't inculcate in our children these qualities of the heart.

Some children abuse and badmouth their parents. But without our parents, we would not be here. Our human birth depends on our parents. When we were born, our parents looked at us and did not say, "Yuck, what a horrible pink worm!" and throw us away. Our parents cleaned us; they changed our nappies; they fed us; they soothed us when we cried. Without our parents we wouldn't be alive today. It doesn't matter how hopeless we might think our parents are. They are human beings and have their good points and failings like everyone else. Our parents were always there for us when we were small, and they loved us. So we owe them an immense debt of gratitude.

And then there are our teachers—we wouldn't be able to read and write or know anything if it were not for these people who taught us, who showed us how to think, how to learn. We should be so grateful. We should really thank them from our hearts for what they gave us. Why are we critical? Society is very difficult, especially with the young nowadays. It has become very demanding, judgmental, and selfish. There is little gratitude.

And third, we can give to those on account of their needs—the poor and the sick, or anyone who is especially needy. It's nice to give your coat to your best friend, but it's more meaningful to give it to someone who doesn't have a coat and is cold. Giving appropriately to those who really are in need is very basic. Sometimes, what people need is just attention. They need someone who hears their pain and doesn't just dismiss it.

The quality of our lives, whether we are closed-hearted or open-hearted, depends on us. Therefore, the first gesture of an open heart is generosity.

Shila paramita, or ethics

The second perfection is *shila paramita*, or ethics. In Sanskrit, *shila* means "ethics"; it means moral conduct. In the Buddhadharma, moral conduct is based on the principle of harmlessness, of not hurting oneself or others. Seen in that way, the precepts laid down by the Buddha are very logical. These are not commandments. He didn't say, "Thou shall not do this; thou shall not do that." The actual wording of the first precept says, "I undertake the rule of training to abstain from the taking of life." It is a rule of training based on the spontaneous and natural conduct of an enlightened being, an *arhat*. A liberated arhat will naturally be incapable of intentionally taking life. We try to model our conduct on the natural conduct of a liberated being, because if we want to build our house, if we want to build our spiritual temple, it's no good just concentrating on the golden roof and the frescoed walls. We have to start by establishing a deep, strong foundation. Any building with a weak foundation is going to crack and fall very soon. It doesn't matter how splendid that golden roof may be. If we want to build a good house, we have to deal with the foundation and the plumbing and all those unromantic essentials. If we have a very good solid foundation, then the house will quite quickly be built.

Our foundations are the qualities of basic ethical conduct that find expression through our way of living in this world. These precepts were laid down 2,500 years ago, but they are eternal. They are not something that was relevant two millennia ago in northern India but no longer appropriate for us now in Australia, Brazil, Italy, the United States, or wherever else. They are relevant in any time, any place, and for any race of people. As mentioned earlier in the chapter on renunciation, these five basic ethical precepts are not to take life, not to take what is not given, not to lie, not to engage in sexual misconduct, and not to indulge in alcohol or drugs which intoxicate the mind. Let us now deepen our exploration of these precepts.

The first precept, and the one most fundamental for living in this world harmlessly, is the precept not to take life. Now that means all lives, not just human lives. It means the lives of animals and insects, including those in the air, on the ground, under the ground, and in the oceans and rivers. Why? Because for each being its own life is most precious. No being wants to be killed. If there was a little ant on this table and I tapped near it with my fingers, it would rear up and run in the other direction. Why? Because in its own way it is thinking, "There is danger! Something might harm me; I must go away from that."

When we take the vow not to harm others, we are saying to the world and to all beings, "You have nothing to fear from me; in my presence, you are safe." It is this basic appreciation for all other beings on this planet which is so fundamental. Even if we don't actually benefit anyone else, at least we don't harm them. Of course, we try to benefit also, but here we are dealing with the question of not harming, not hurting anything. We human beings are really a problem for this planet. Imagine: some insect comes by, and if we don't like it we just squish it with no thought that this being has its own life with its joys and sorrows. We don't know what kind of world it is experiencing. What right have we to just terminate its life?

In this imperfect world, we may not always keep this precept perfectly because as the Buddha himself said, this world is covered with much dust. It is a very dusty world, and dust is falling continually. There are always compromises which we have to make, but we must be very careful with our compromises and not justify them easily. As much as we possibly can we should really try to become whole by conducting ourselves with integrity. Most of the time, we can do that. We can learn not to see situations solely from the angle of our own convenience if we make the effort. Other creatures have their point of view. I am not going into the whole field of animal rights, but animals *do* have rights. Insects have rights. We all have rights and we should think about that. We should think about living in this world so as not to keep trampling on everything all the time. Let us tread a little more gently. When I was first with my lama, he said, "I want you to take just one precept. Consider that you have all the others, but take just one first." I chose this one, not taking life, and he said that was the right thing to do. Because this precept is fundamental to all the others.

The second ethical precept concerns not taking that which is not given. It's a little bit more specific than not stealing, which is what it means, of course. In the monastic sangha, they take this very seriously. For example, there was a Catholic nun who once brought me several tins of processed cheese from Delhi. This was in the mid-1960s, and in those days processed cheese was very rare in India. I decided to offer the cheese to my lama, Khamtrul Rinpoche, but as he didn't happen to be there, I put the tins on his desk, right in front of where he sat, so he could see that they were for him. He came back, days went by, and the tins of cheese were still sitting there, stacked up like the Tower of Pisa. Eventually I said to him, "Rinpoche, why don't you take that cheese? Don't you like it?" And he replied, "Well, I thought they were for me because they're sitting there, but you haven't offered them." So I picked up the tins of cheese and handed them to him and said, "They are yours." But that's the point. Integrity here is also linked with this question of harmlessness—people know that their property is safe with us.

Books—who has ever lent a book and waved it goodbye? And what about videos, CDs, and DVDs? Returning something we've borrowed, and in as good a condition as when we got it, is a matter of integrity. Why? Because at our level of realization, we still identify ourselves with what we own, and we don't like it when people simply take what is ours.

During the hippie period in the 1960s and early 1970s there were those who felt that "everybody's property is my property." They didn't believe in private ownership, but what happened? Maybe in the early days there really was a sense of free-flowing ownership. But in the end they held to the attitude of "what you own is mine and what I own is mine too." It was not an especially open-hearted attitude. They would stay on somebody else's property, and when the owners wanted to evict them, they didn't say, "Well, that's fair enough, because everything belongs to everybody." They said, "No, now it's mine." We have to be careful of this grasping quality of mind. This precept of not taking what is not given respects these boundaries. Obviously, not killing and not stealing are fundamental to a well-ordered society.

Another ethical precept, not engaging in sexual misconduct, basically refers to any kind of sexual activity which could bring harm to oneself or to another. This is an especially relevant question nowadays because people are often extremely irresponsible sexually; sex has often been used merely as a means for self-gratification, and with no thought of either the physical or the emotional consequences. But sex is not like having an ice-cream when we are feeling greedy. It is a dialogue. It is a relationship, even if it is only a one-night stand. Yet we deal with such fundamental energy in irresponsible ways.

We are often very immature when it comes to sexual relationships. We act like fifteen-year-olds even if we are fifty, or even seventy. We have all seen it. Look at the politicians or the big celebrities. They have so much to lose, so much at stake, but yet they act like school kids. It's pathetic, and it reflects the real state of inner immaturity and their lack of responsibility to themselves, their families, and society. We have to ask ourselves, "Why am I doing this? Is it just because—right now—I want this gratification?" We should ask ourselves about possible repercussions this action could have on ourselves and on others. Could it cause unwanted pregnancies? How many abortions are caused by irresponsible sexuality? It's not like this isn't a problem anymore. It's not as though we have solved this through contraception, because so many abortions are still performed. And what about the big problem of rampant sexually transmitted diseases?

It is not just the physical side. There is also the emotional aspect to be considered. Any kind of sexual activity which causes damage in any way to anyone is not wholesome. Sexual activity should be an expression of caring, of love, and not just an outlet for lust, greed, and exploitation. Recently I went to visit a women's prison and I was told that at least eighty percent of the women who come into this prison had suffered sexual abuse as children, most of it incestuous. So this is not an irrelevant issue. Our irresponsibility in sexual areas destroys life. These women were inwardly mutilated and they later indulged in a lot of very harmful and self-destructive behavior because of their hatred of themselves due to the abuse in childhood. So many women I meet out in the world, and not just in prison, have exactly the same problems. So we must be very careful to not merely utilize the other person for our pleasure and gratification, but use love-making as an expression of genuine care.

The next precept for us to contemplate is lying. And lying doesn't just mean telling untruths: it actually includes all unwholesome speech. Wholesome skillful speech should be truthful, kind, and helpful. There are many people who pride themselves on their honest speech and claim to say what is on their mind. But it is surprising how often this approach is just a channel or vent for their negativities—the anger, the ill-will, and the jealousy in their minds. We must be very careful because our speech really influences others.

We have a saying, "Sticks and stones may break my bones, but words can never harm me." But that is very idealistic. The Tibetans have a saying, too: "Swords can only harm the flesh, but harsh words can tear a man's heart to pieces." That is so true.

We as human beings have this very rare gift of communication through speech, but we tend to use it too casually. Often we say certain things in a moment of irritation; we don't really mean it, but it just comes out. People hold that in their hearts, and they remember.

But it is not only a question of not harming—it is also a matter of growing up. The Buddha called unliberated people like us "the children." In English, this is sometimes translated as "fools." The actual word means "childish" or "immature," and that's what we are regardless of what age we may be. Some children are much wiser than their parents, though not always. But our level of childishness is also a mark of irresponsibility, and we have to grow up and take responsibility for our lives. A mature person is someone who is integrated and whose thoughts are centered not on themselves but on others.

The fifth ethical precept concerns alcohol. Why was that included in the list? Presumably any thinking person knows the answer to that. Under the influence of alcohol, our negative impulses emerge. When someone gets drunk, they don't go out and join Mother Teresa. They are more likely to go home and beat up their wives and children or get in their cars and drive irresponsibly and crash or run someone over. Alcohol not only destroys our minds, it destroys our bodies. I know it is difficult in society for many of you to give up all alcohol and so one cannot ask that. But I can say, at least try to reduce your intake of drinks, and never get to the point where your mind is seriously affected. It would benefit you and those around you. It would benefit society.

Nothing is more boring than someone who is drunk. They may think they are brilliant, but a person who is sober just thinks, "Get me out of here." Being inebriated is pathetic. It's not clever, and it's not sophisticated, no matter what the advertising tries to tell us. Of course, alcohol companies want us to think that alcohol is very stylish and classy, but that's just because they want us to buy their product. People who are addicted to alcohol, cigarettes, or drugs are slaves. We can be enslaved through terror or we can be enslaved through pleasure, but it is still enslavement.

Actions which in our ordinary sober mind we would never consider often become feasible and seem desirable when we are in this other state of consciousness brought on by alcohol or drugs. People do things which they would never dream of doing if they were sober. If inebriation brought out really good, positive qualities, it might be okay, but it does not. So much of the violence and the abuse in society occur because people are drunk or they are stoned on drugs. The World Health Organization says that more than one-third of the disease burden in the world has its basis in alcohol consumption. So this is not a minor precept which we can forget. All I can say is, please, if you are trying to live a life which is spiritually based, then take it seriously.

The Buddhist path is the way of increasing clarity of mind and increasing inward control so that we are not enslaved by our thoughts and our feelings but are masters of our interior world. Alcohol goes in the opposite direction. It is totally counterproductive. If one cannot abstain completely, at least one should try to cut one's consumption down to acceptable levels. A glass of wine at dinner, okay. Maybe one glass of beer with someone you meet at the pub. But three or four or five glasses is not all right.

Kshanti paramita, or patience

In ancient India there was a kind of austerity known in Sanskrit as *tapasya*, and we can see this at work in many other spiritual traditions. *Tapasya* often took the form of very severe fasting. For example, the Buddha himself fasted until he was only eating a single grain of rice a day. Other forms of austerity would include standing for years with one arm in the air, or never sitting down at all, or standing on one foot, or standing out in the Indian summer in the midst of four fires with the sun above as the fifth fire. These are things which people do, even today. But the Buddha said to forget them all except for the greatest austerity, *kshanti paramita*, which is patience. Now, this sense of austerity means having patience and tolerance toward difficult people, trying circumstances, and adverse conditions. Patience expresses a mind that is very open and spacious.

Consider how each one of us is just one person. There is one "me" while in this whole world there are billions of "non-me"s. Are we going to spend our lives trying to make everybody say and do exactly what we want them to say and do in order that we may be peaceful? This is not feasible. As Shantideva reminds us in the *Bodhicharyavatara (Way of the Bodhisattva)*, the earth is full of stones and thorns, and as we walk around we are bound to stub our toes on the sharp flints. So what are we going to do? he asks. Are we going to carpet the whole world so that it will be soft underfoot? This is not possible, even with all the money in the world. But there is no need to go to such extremes. All we require is a piece of leather beneath our soles in the form of sandals or shoes and then we can walk anywhere. Likewise, we cannot create a world in which all circumstances and all beings act in accordance with our wishes. It's exhausting to even think about it! But if we arm our own mind with patience and tolerance, then we can deal with everyone and every situation.

Anger is a very interesting emotion. Going around from east to west and north to south in whatever country in the world, I am asked two main questions. One question is, "How do I find a spiritual master?" People generally ask this out of a need for guidance. But there are some who ask out of the fantasy that if they could only meet a certain spiritual master, somehow or other all their problems would be solved. They don't understand that that's probably when their problems actually begin! And the second question which is asked again and again is, "How do I deal with anger?" Because anger is an unpleasant feeling. We don't like to be angry—it makes us feel uncomfortable. People don't like us; they don't admire us when we are angry. So we want to rid ourselves of it. In a way, we much prefer to indulge an emotion we enjoy. We don't want to be rid of clinging and greed, provided that our greed is sometimes fulfilled. We like desiring things as long as we sometimes get the objects of our desire. Desire is a much harder emotion to transform because we like it, and we don't really want to get rid of it. Anger, on the whole, is universally understood to be negative. The Buddha said that while karmically anger was at least eight times heavier than attachment, it is much easier to eradicate because we don't like it. We are happy to be rid of it.

There are various levels through which we can approach the subject of patience, but first we must understand that we can change—we can change our attitude. For example, instead of seeing someone we don't like as a problem, we could try to see that they are actually a great opportunity for us to learn. We need to have difficult circumstances and difficult people in our lives in order to cultivate patience, and we can't cultivate this quality if we don't have anyone or anything challenging us. If we continually meet people who are very kind and loving, friendly and helpful, that is absolutely wonderful, but we can get kind of flabby spiritually.

Patience can be a problem for me because usually people are very nice to me. One can get lulled into a false sense of one's own niceness because it is very easy to be pleasant to people who are kind. But then, if I walk into an Indian government office, and the officials are obnoxious, then we can see it. Right, there it is. Anger has not gone away. Then we can decide either to be rude in return, or we can think, "Wow, thank you." This is the opportunity— right now—to transform the situation and not answer back in the obvious way.

We can really value the fact that we can meet people who are being difficult and obstreperous as spiritual friends—they are our spiritual helpers on the path because without them, we could never learn to develop patience and tolerance and loving-kindness. It is easy to be loving toward someone who is lovable. The challenge is to be loving to someone who is absolutely horrible.

In Buddhist cosmology there are many levels of beings. But the human realm is considered ideal because we supposedly have intelligence and we also have choice. We have the balance between pain and pleasure: enough pain to keep us awake and enough pleasure so that we don't totally despair. We have to appreciate that and not always look for everything to be just lovely. And so when things do go wrong, when we do meet people who are difficult, instead of falling into despair or trying to run away or drug ourselves into not acknowledging it, we make use of that situation. We make use of it through our intelligence.

Patience isn't something passive—it is very active and very intelligent. It is important, in all circumstances, to have this kind of openness, so that when things go well we can be happy, but when things don't go so well we can still be okay. We can deal with it. We learn through patience to be as stable as a mountain. We don't shake, whatever winds are blowing against us. The first book I ever read on Buddhism was called *Mind Unshaken: A Modern Approach to Buddhism,* by John Walters; I started to read it just because I liked the title. It talks about a mind that is unshaken by pleasure, unshaken by pain—a fearless mind. Usually we live our whole lives trying to avoid pain and attract pleasure; we are afraid that we will experience more pain than pleasure. This creates a very insecure and fearful mind, because we know that we cannot have one without the other. But we can face everything within a spacious yet grounded mind. When we deal skillfully with both the pleasure and the pain, where is the fear? There is no hope and fear in that kind of mind. Whatever comes, we can deal with it; whoever comes, we can deal with them.

I want to express this clearly because I don't want you to think that culti-vating patience just means being weak and passive and unable to answer back or stand firm. It's not that. Someone who is patient and doesn't hit back is much stronger than the person who hits. Movies unfortunately tend to model a very macho culture where if someone annoys us, we just bash him, or kick him in the face, or blow him up, and that's the solution. But of course that is not the solution to anything, as we know very well. If something upsets us and annoys us, maybe we should really look into our own mind. In the movie *Star Wars*, there is one scene where Luke Skywalker gets angry as he faces the Dark Emperor. He begins to verbally abuse him, saying that he would always be against him and his evil ways and so on. And the Dark Emperor says, "Yes, go for it. Get angry. Hate me. Work to destroy me because as long as you are angry toward me, as long as you hate me, you are on our side." Now that was very profound. Of course after that the characters are fighting and blowing each other up again. But what the Dark Emperor said was actually very true.

Patience is a great strength. It is not a weakness. The ability to use anger as an aid on the path is an incredible strength. Instead of becoming angry, instead of losing control, one can transform the anger. There are many ways. One method is to understand that the person who makes us angry is our greatest spiritual benefactor, and far from being upset with them, we should be grateful. Another way beyond that is being able to make use of the anger itself, but that is quite difficult, and so I will not discuss it here.

We miss so much in our lives if we are unable to deal with discomfort. There was a group of devotees who went to visit a high lama who has since passed away in Nepal. He lived up on the hill behind Bodhnath Stupa. The students arrived at his monastery one evening, and the following day they were to begin receiving a full week of teachings. He was a lama especially skillful in pointing out the inherent nature of mind, so they were very lucky.

The next day, when the interpreter went to the monastery to translate for them, the lama said, "Well, actually they have left."

The translator said, "Why did they leave? Where did they go?"

The lama replied, "Well, they didn't like the bathrooms." He sighed and said, "Dharma good, toilets no good!"

The group had left. The students lost this unique opportunity to get teach-ing because they didn't have any tolerance. I was there and I can't even remember the toilet, so it couldn't have been that bad!

We have to deal with our inability to put up with a little bit of discomfort, to put up with the difficulties of other people around us. Now when we are cultivating the practice of taking the Dharma into our everyday life, where better to exercise this practice of patience than with our family, our colleagues, and people we deal with every day? On the whole it's easier to be patient and understanding with strangers, but our real challenge comes from the people who are close to us. Some of you, I am sure, get on beautifully with your families. You never have any arguments, everything is complete bliss and joy, and it is as if you were in the realm of celestials. That is wonderful, but for the rest of us....

One of the problems in families is that we do get locked into unhealthy patterns from which we are unable to extricate ourselves. So it is really important to develop the quality of standing back and observing the situation by seeing and hearing ourselves. But to see and hear ourselves accurately we have to take into account the tone of our voice. We may think later, "Oh, but I only said this and this and this." Yet perhaps it wasn't what we said but rather how we said it that brought difficulty. We need to be aware of our tone of voice, the way we act, our body language. And we need to pay attention to the way we relate to children, and how we may affect the way children relate to themselves—it is all interconnected. This is our field of practice. This is where we have to transform.

It's no good having love and kindness for the rest of the world if we cannot deal with those who are closest to us. We have to start where we are. For some reason, we have some karmic relationships—we are interconnected, we are responsible for each other. Sometimes, there are partners who are mismatched and it would obviously be better if they parted. I don't mean that couples have to stay together forever and ever, just because it is a way of practicing patience. But nonetheless, while one is in any kind of relationship, even if one is going to separate, this is the opportunity to learn and develop, to cultivate and create something more positive, even when a situation has become very negative. We do not necessarily need to ditch the whole thing and say, "Let's try again somewhere else," nor just carry on because we are too tired and worn down to think of how to get out of it.

We all have the possibility for change. It does not matter how long something has been going on—our ways of acting and speaking—we can change. When something is not right, when something is negative, when something is out of balance, then this is our opportunity to really try to bring it back into balance again. After all, if there is estrangement between two people, originally there must have been some care involved. So then, what went wrong? This is our area of practice. This is where we can really learn what is going on within us. We do not need to put the blame all on the other, nor do we need to put the blame all on ourselves. We just need to see the situation clearly. Then we can decide whether or not something can be done.

Every situation we meet in life is an area for our practice. It is where we have to work. It is not glamorous. It is not romantic. It is not esoteric and exotic. But it is where we can learn in this lifetime. We are all where we are right now because of causes which we ourselves have created. And so what are we going to do? It is up to us.

Virya paramita, or effort

Contemplating *virya paramita*, or the perfection of effort, leads us to the question of enthusiastic energy. Does the idea itself make you feel exhausted? We never can accomplish anything if we don't really try, if we don't have some ongoing perseverance. On the spiritual path, the two qualities most needed are patience and perseverance. For instance, many people who want to meditate do sit down but after only two or three sessions they say, "Oh, I can't meditate. Too many thoughts." And they give up. Nothing worthwhile was ever accomplished without diligence, without perseverance, without effort. When they train for the Olympics, athletes are completely one-pointed. They change their diet and give up smoking and alcohol. They get up early; they go to bed early. They train the whole day long. Everything else is sacrificed. And for what? To get a medal.

In Buddhism, laziness is described as being of three types. First, there is the laziness that says, "Yes, I like going to the Dharma center, I like meditating, but there is a really good movie on television, so sorry." It is the kind of laziness in which we have lots of enthusiasm for something that we really want to do, but when it comes to meditation or any kind of serious Dharma reading, suddenly we find ourselves saying, "Oh goodness, I am so tired. I'll do my practice later when I have time." It is the kind of laziness in which we remember what a late night we had the night before, and that's the end of that. We all suffer from this gross kind of laziness, which is easy to recognize.

The second kind of laziness is the laziness that comes when we are unable to practice because we feel so unworthy. The conviction that everyone else but me can practice and meditate and get realizations—"I can't because I always fail at everything; I did try to meditate but I couldn't do it because I have too many thoughts"—that is laziness. The sense that we can't do the practice because of this or that is not regarded as humility but rather as gross laziness. We are shirking. We all have buddha nature; all we have to do is to discover it. Therefore, it is not a question of being higher or lower or unworthy. Unworthy of what? We all have the potential of being enlightened; we all have this human birth; we all have some intelligence.

The third kind of laziness refers to being so busy with mundane activities, even Dharma activities, that we have no time for inner cultivation. Whatever excuse we make to ourselves does not matter. If we find ourselves filling up our days with things to do week after week, month after month, year after year, we never have time to go inside. Even if we are like rodents on a wheel, that is still laziness. We are avoiding the real task. Our task here is first to realize our own innate buddha nature, and anything which takes us away from that is just avoidance.

And this is why it is so important that we use the events of our day as a way of cultivating an open heart and clarity of mind. Outwardly some activities may look very good, like running Dharma centers and things like this, but even they can be an excuse for not really facing what we are here for. A genuine spiritual aspirant is like a marathon runner, not a short distance runner. It is very easy in the beginning to have lots of enthusiasm. We can see people bubbling over with enthusiasm in Dharma centers: they throw themselves into all the practices and into all the activities. They are so bright and starry-eyed and joyful. And we can see them, ten years down the road, still going. Fifteen years along the way, they have begun to slow down a bit. By the time they are twenty to twenty-five years down the line, they are saying, "Wow, I used to be so enthusiastic, but now, somehow, I have lost my interest. How do I get enthusiastic again?" That is a difficult one.

The quality of perseverance beyond the initial spurt of enthusiasm is invaluable. The ability to keep going, even when the going is not exciting anymore and nothing much is happening inwardly, is such an important quality. In old translations they sometimes used the word "manliness" for the Sanskrit word we're translating as "effort," *virya*. In Latin, the word for man is *vir*. Sanskrit and Latin are connected, and those donnish scholars were thinking "man" as expressive of carrying on with the task—get on with it!

The muscular Christianity type of approach. Then they translated *virya* as determination, perseverance, effort, but as most people probably felt tired just reading about that, later translators started calling it enthusiasm, which sounded a bit more upbeat. What it means is not just enthusiasm, but also this sense of carrying on, like a marathon runner. Marathon runners keep back a lot of their strength so that they can keep going; they don't expend all their energy in the first thousand meters because they know they've got miles and miles to go yet. So they manage their energy very carefully and keep on track and learn how to breathe properly and how to pace themselves so that they can just keep going.

The perfection of effort is this quality of being able to keep the momentum going, day after day after month after year. The good news is that, unlike the marathon runner, once we really begin to see that daily life is our field of practice, and that everything we do and every encounter we have is an opportunity for developing our inner qualities—our loving-kindness, our understanding, our patience, our generosity, our openness of heart—we begin to develop the quality of mindfulness or awareness, and the momentum builds so that we are carried along. Our days become more and more vivid and fulfilling. When that actually happens, and one feels that one is in the flow, so to speak, then one is on the right track. Everyone has better days and not such good days, but basically, if our days feel routine and dull, we haven't got the point. Because if we take everything that we do as a way of cultivating the path step by step, moment by moment, then how could our days be boring? Our understanding of the path gathers its own momentum as we practice, and our responses become more and more skillful automatically. Perseverance in this sense isn't a panting sort of fatigue. It isn't something arduous. It is self-renewing, moment to moment. Once we get on the right track we don't have to generate the energy, as the energy generates itself because we are in balance. This is very important.

Dhyana paramita, or meditation

Let us now look at *dhyana paramita*, or the perfection of meditation. Basically, meditation is divided into two streams: *shamatha*, or calm abiding, which we'll discuss here, and *vipashyana*, or insight, which is traditionally explained in relation to the last of the six perfections, the perfection of wisdom.

Outwardly and inwardly, we only can know anything through our mind.

We experience everything through our mind. If our mind is not functioning, we are more or less dead, or like a zombie. Everything that we experience and know, we experience and know through our six senses. Our six senses are not only the five usual senses but include the mind, meaning that all things which we think are processed through the mind. And yet how many of us have any idea of what the mind is? How many of us experience this mind itself? We are always looking outwards, and even when we talk about the mind, we talk about it from the intellectual point of view. We hear all sorts of theories, ideas, and kinds of psychology, but we almost never even ask ourselves what it is to experience a thought as a thought, an emotion as an emotion. And yet everything—our joys and sorrows, our hopes and fears—everything that we experience and could possibly experience, we can only experience through the mind.

Mindfulness

Before we look at meditation in more detail, it is useful to discuss mindfulness, which in the context of the perfections is technically a factor contributing to the development of shamatha. However, it can also be understood more generally as a quality of awareness that we can develop in daily life to very great benefit. So although in this sense it's not strictly part of the paramitas, I would like to deepen our inquiry here into how we can incorporate this spiritual practice into our daily lives.

What does mindfulness mean? "Mindfulness," in Sanskrit, is *smriti*, and in Tibetan, *drenpa*. They both have the same meaning, which is "to remember." This is very close to the Catholic idea of recollection, or the idea of self-remembrance. It is the quality of being here and now which usually is exactly where we are not. Normally, we are not even aware that we are here or that we are half-here and half-somewhere else. It is extraordinary how unaware we are of our minds. In Buddhism the practice of mindfulness is also connected with positive states of mind. For example, a bank robber might be very attentive and conscious of his actions, but that would not strictly be considered mindfulness because his motivation is unwholesome and based on greed and desire.

Once we start training in mindfulness, we see how totally out of control our minds actually are. One of the ways to learn is to try to be here now. If we say, "Be aware of the body in this moment; just know it," then in that moment, we can know it, we can feel it—we don't judge it but rather just know it. But when we think, "That's easy! Look, I am aware of my body; I am being mindful; I know what this is all about," we have already lost it. Because then we are just *thinking* of being mindful, and we are not mindful anymore. So it's tricky.

This quality of being attentive to what we are doing in the moment is so important because the present moment is all we have. Everything else is past, gone. Our future has not yet come. The only thing happening is this present moment, which is going so fast that we have almost lost it before it is even here. It is flowing, right? It wouldn't matter if it happened that we weren't present only sometimes, but the fact is that we are not present for most of our lives. We are present for a few seconds and then we are off again. And therefore our lives become very dull, routine and boring. The French have an expression for being bored—*je m'ennuie*—which means literally, "I bore myself." Exactly. It has nothing to do with what is going on around us. Our minds bore us.

Let us address how we can be present. Because if we can learn how to develop some basic mindfulness, then that will enliven everything, everything that we do during the day. This is very important, so don't fall asleep!

Thich Nhat Hanh, a Vietnamese Zen master, talks about two ways to wash the dishes. One way is to wash the dishes to get clean dishes; and the other way is to wash dishes to wash dishes. Now normally when we wash dishes, as with any activity we do, we want a result. We wash dishes to have clean dishes, and then we go on to the next task. The actual task of washing the dishes in itself is irrelevant. As we are washing the dishes, we are thinking. We are thinking of what was said this morning at breakfast, or we're thinking of last night's television program, or we're thinking, "Well, after this, I'll have some coffee and then I'll have to go to the supermarket—what do I need?" Or we're thinking about something we are going to do that evening, or we're caught up in some fantasy world, or whatever. The one thing we are not thinking about is those dishes. Right? And when we have finished washing the dishes, which are now clean and stacked up, we've got to drink our coffee, and have a slice of chocolate cake. We drink the coffee. We are usually fairly conscious of the first sip; we judge whether we like it or we don't like it. But already, by the second sip, we are not really conscious of it. And by the third sip, we are totally unaware that we are drinking the coffee because we're thinking of what we have to buy at the supermarket, that is, before the memory from years ago slips in, "and then he said *that* to me and I said *this* to him…" When we eat the chocolate cake or something else that is nice, we decide the first bite is yummy, by the second bite we have already lost interest, and by the third bite we are munching away and don't even know it. Our whole life is led like that.

One meaning of the word *buddha* is "to wake up." He is the Awakened One. He awoke from the dream of ignorance. But the rest of us are still dreaming. Good dreams or nightmares—it's all a dream. We're somnambulists. We look very bright, but we're asleep. Where are our minds? I sometimes really think it would be very interesting—horrible, but interesting—to have loudspeakers attached to our minds, so that everyone could hear our thoughts. Wouldn't everybody want to know how to meditate quickly?! Because when we look inside and see what is going on in our mind, we find endless chatter, endless trivia, and it is not even entertaining. If we really watch it, we see how totally boring it is. The same old stale thoughts, opinions, and memories are constantly recycled. And while we're prattling away to ourselves we have the radio on or the television yapping in the background. There is no silence. Mindfulness is about being silent. It is about having a mind which is completely quiet and present with what is happening.

The other way to wash dishes is to wash dishes to wash dishes. This way we still get clean dishes. But when we wash the dishes like this, we are doing the most important thing that we could possibly be doing, right now. We are washing the dishes. It is what we are doing. This is the moment. If we miss this, it is gone. Alert, conscious of the water and of one's hands and of the dishes, one can know that and just be present. That sense of presence, of knowing, is the vital point. Because if we can really learn how to do that, then when we've washed the dishes, we've not only washed the dishes, we've washed our mind. We have a nice, clean, and sparkling mind along with the dishes. It is very easy. But the problem is that we forget. The real meaning of mindfulness is to remember, and its direct enemy is forgetfulness.

The inertia of our mind is so great. Sometimes when people hear about mindfulness, they think, "Well, this sounds good, let's have a go." They really try to be present with what they're doing. They try to hear themselves when they speak, and know what they are thinking; they try to be present and know how they are moving and how they are here, in the moment, as much as possible. When we first start, mostly we are just thinking about being present, and this is quite difficult. We proceed from where we are.

People try to be present, and then they say, "Well that was great, I really enjoyed today. I've been trying now for two or three days, and it's really fun to be mindful. My friends are already saying I'm a much nicer person and I feel really good. This is great."

And we think, "Oh yes, just wait."

In six weeks' time we inquire into how the mindfulness is coming along. "The mindfulness?... Oops, forgot!"

Forgot. Not because it wasn't working. Not because it was impossibly difficult. Actually, mindfulness is reasonably easy. But the inertia and the laziness of our mind, the reluctance of our mind to be in the present, is very deep.

The Buddha said that mindfulness was like salt in curries. In other words, it is what gives taste to everything that we do. It brings everything alive, because it is as though we are doing it for the first time. The world becomes vivid and clear. Normally, it is like we're looking through a lens and it's all blurred. We cannot see clearly. So it is with the mind. But once we adjust the lens, suddenly everything comes into focus and appears newly washed, like those dishes, and not like the stale old mind that we normally live with. This is a new mind. This quality of mindfulness is very important in developing the spiritual qualities of our daily lives. And it is something which we can all cultivate during the day and night.

The Buddha divided mindfulness into four aspects: mindfulness of the body; mindfulness of the feelings; mindfulness of the mind itself; and in the Mahayana interpretation, mindfulness of external dharmas or phenomena. That means everything received through the five senses—sights, sounds, tastes, touch, and smells.

Let us start with mindfulness of the body. The body is the most tangible of the aspects. The Tibetans usually emphasize mindfulness of the mind itself but that is quite difficult at this first stage since our minds are very fast-flowing and turbulent and difficult to catch hold of. Maybe it is better to start with something fairly stable and solid, like our bodies. The Buddha says we start by thinking, "When I am standing, I know I am standing; when I am sitting, I know I am sitting; when I am lying down, I know I am lying down; when I am walking, I know I am walking."

Just think about that. How often do we stand or sit without even being conscious that we are standing or sitting because our minds are racing ahead? Normally we don't even know what our bodies are doing. And yet this is something very simple to bring into the present—just to know we are sitting as we are sitting. Experience how the body feels in the moment: this is bodily awareness. Become aware of the breath. Consciously breathing in and breathing out is a way to become instantly centered. We cannot breathe in the past or in the future—we can only breathe now.

There are infinite opportunities throughout the day to practice mindfulness of the body. Some years ago in New Delhi, on the red stop traffic lights, they had written across them in big white letters, *RELAX*. When we come to a red light we relax and breathe in, and breathe out, feeling gratitude to the light for being red, and for giving us the opportunity to become centered again. If we ring somebody up and all we get is their interminable answering machine, great—we breathe in, and breathe out, becoming centered, and by that time, we are ready to give our message after the tone. Throughout the day there are endless opportunities to come back into our center, into our conscious being—brushing teeth, eating and drinking, combing our hair, shaving, whatever. Use that moment, that simple action—and know it, in that moment. Don't brush your teeth and think of a thousand other things. Just brush your teeth to brush your teeth, and know. It is all training in being present. Because the present is all we have.

If we learn how to really use our day to develop this quality of mindfulness and awareness, then when we come to sit for meditation, there won't be such problems. Instead of the mind being nothing but a hindrance, we are using it to help us. Those of you who are serious about cultivating this practice should read books on the subject, and if possible, attend meditation courses and inquire from those who have greater experience in this quality of mindfulness. Because it is a very important quality, and it has nothing to do with one's spiritual orientation. Everyone can use it. And during this most profound practice, nobody even knows we're practicing! We can carry it with us everywhere under any circumstances, even onto the toilet. It doesn't matter where—every action, every thought, and every word can be an object of our awareness, of our knowing.

Shamatha, or calm abiding

Usually, our minds are very agitated by the six senses—by sights, sounds, smells, tastes, touch, and by the sixth sense of mind itself, with its thoughts, judgments, memories, ideas, and opinions. All this churns up the mind continually. And because of this, we do not see things clearly. We do not reflect the external environment as it really is. We only get our version, our interpretation of what is happening, which is distorted by all this turmoil that is going on inside us. We respond only to our rendition, our interpretation of what is happening, not to the actuality itself. When we try to look into the mind itself, it is so churned up that we cannot yet look beyond the surface thoughts, the surface chatter. Through shamatha meditation, the mind begins to quieten down. The outer senses are no longer so reactive. And the inner sixth sense, the mind itself, becomes very tranquil, calm, and one-pointed. It becomes clear. And when it is clear the mind sees very accurately because it is no longer interpreting. At the same time, we are able to use that calm, one-pointed mind to look in on itself and see through increasingly subtle layers of the psyche. Therefore, this first attaining of a state of calm, single-pointedness is really quite important. One lama said to me that if we have a good shamatha practice, then all the Dharma is in the palm of our hands.

Whatever practice we are doing, if we do it with a distracted mind then it is not going to work. There are books that tell us that even if we were to say a mantra for one hundred aeons, if we say it with a distracted mind we would not accomplish the goal. But if we say even a few mantras with a mind that is really concentrated and merged in the practice, then results will come very quickly. Therefore, it is worthwhile to train our mind—as much as we can—to become quiet, focused, and calm. This is stage number one. Our practice does not end here.

When the Buddha left his palace to seek answers to the causes and problems of suffering, he first studied under two yogis. Now these yogis were teaching a kind of shamatha practice. Traditionally, in shamatha practice, there are many levels: there are lower material levels, and there are higher formless, or immaterial, levels. In these formless levels, there is no thinking as such. There is infinity of space, infinity of consciousness, neither perception nor non-perception, and nothing whatsoever. It is a very refined state of mind, and it is the ultimate state of nothingness. There is neither consciousness nor no consciousness. During the Buddha's time, this was regarded as liberation. The Buddha accomplished this state quickly, but he said it was not liberation, as this state was still within the realm of birth and death. The practitioner had not gone beyond. And so he left those yogis and wandered forth.

So why is this not liberation? This kind of meditation, although very important as preparation, if indulged in too much could be counterproductive. Sometimes practitioners enter into blissful states and think they are liberated; everything is so clear. But what can happen is that the state of

bliss can act as a shield which hides one's negative emotions. One's delusions, greed, lust, anger, and ill-will are all still lying latent. This is very
dangerous because it deludes us into thinking that we are much more spiritually advanced than we are and that all our negative emotions have been
eradicated. We can imagine that we no longer have any negative emotions
because we are in this state of bliss and clarity where everything is one and
it is all very wonderful. We look, and we can't see anything negative because
it has been covered up; but the defilements are all there, growing underneath, and if the opportunity arises, they erupt, often uncontrollably. These
negative emotions are intensified because the mind has become so powerful. Although these delusions have been covered over, when they do erupt,
they are that much more dangerous than they could ever be in an ordinary
untrained mind. There are many troubling contemporary examples of this
amongst certain gurus, but these situations are usually concealed by their
disciples. We can get into this state where all seems absolutely perfect, but
actually the deeply rooted problem has never been resolved. When it comes
back again, it is all the more difficult to control.

There is also the problem of remaining in and being attached to the state
of calmness. We can get attached to anything, and this is ultimately an obstacle. However, as the first step, it is very important to develop this quality of
getting the mind calmed down and one-pointed. There are many ways of
doing this. It is important when we start to meditate that it not be regarded
as a kind of endurance test.

We can think of the mind as being like a wild horse, and there are basically
two ways to deal with the problem of taming it. We can catch it and beat
it into submission, forcing it to carry out our own will, and eventually the
horse will break down and become docile. What we have then is a broken
hack which is sad and resentful. Sometimes in India we can see such horses.
They're pulling carriages, and we know that is the way they've been treated.
They are very unhappy, dejected animals who try whatever they can to get
away from their labors but they get beaten back into submission again. However, there is another way. We can try to tame the horse through more gentle
means by slowly, enticingly, and gradually trying to win the horse's good will.
Quieting the horse's fear, we let him know that nothing bad will happen.
Patiently we win him over, until eventually he begins to trust us, willing from
his side to do what we want.

Likewise, there are two approaches to taming the mind. One is that we really force the mind through long sitting sessions, not moving for a moment, and coercing it into being concentrated. And that can work. Either we get a mind which maybe never wants to meditate again or our mind feels so triumphant from having been able to sit and concentrate, unmoving, for hours and hours on end that it is willing to go on.

But generally it is more skillful the way my teacher taught, which is to win the cooperation of the mind. If we are watching an interesting movie or television program, or if we are reading a fascinating book, nobody has to coerce us into concentrating. We are there, we are absorbed, we are merged with it, the hours go by and we haven't even noticed. Our mind is very one-pointed.

We all have the capacity to be one-pointed and absorbed, concentrated on one stream of events. Our challenge is to bring that kind of interest and absorption into something which is not initially absolutely fascinating, like observing the in-going and out-going of the breath, minute after minute, hour after hour, day after day, year after year.

Therefore, if one has never practiced much before, it is a good idea to start with short sessions. This is because when we actually start meditating, if we begin to get more concentrated and calm then that's fine. If we stop just when we are still enjoying the practice and we could still go a little bit more, then our minds remember that that was fun and we are willing to try again. If we push too far, then the mind becomes tired and we lose our concentration. If we keep pushing, the next time when we sit, the mind will remember that it felt tired and bored and there will be a sense of aversion. We are not trying to battle the mind. This is not a matter of subjugation, of beating down the mind until it finally obeys. It is a matter of encouraging the mind to cooperate and to realize that there is genuine happiness in being calm, one-pointed, and clear. The initial difficulties are the inner distractions which we experience, which are really no problem as they can be utilized as part of the process.

People imagine that when they sit down to meditate they should immediately be able to access deep levels of silence, calm, and one-pointedness, but when they sit down and discover that they seem to have more thoughts than normal, they become very discouraged. Everybody more or less experiences the same problems. I am sure even the Lord Buddha himself never just sat down and immediately had no thoughts. If that had been so, he could never have taught meditation because he wouldn't have known the problems. But as he talked so much about the difficulties of meditation, it seems he must have experienced them.

Everyone has problems, everyone has difficulties, and those who are finally accomplished are those who persevere. But sometimes, if we feel we can't do it, it helps to keep the sessions not too long. We practice, and then rest the mind, and start again; we practice, and then rest the mind, and start again. Gradually, the mind begins to acclimatize. It's like physical exercises. If we want to do yoga or aerobics and we start off by doing a two-hour session and we have never exercised before, then we either collapse during the session, or else we are unable to move the next day. Of course we can't move because everything aches! We think, "Oh yoga, don't even mention that." We don't want to try again. But if we do a short session, stretching as far as we can but not too far, we think, "That's not too bad, let's try again." We carry on, and the sessions get longer and longer, and before we know it, those exercises which the more advanced yoga students were doing and which seemed so impossible, suddenly we can do them, too.

Why should it not be the same with the mind which is totally untrained? Of course at the beginning there will be problems and resistance. So we need to be skillful. We need to reassure the mind. "This is genuine refuge for the mind. This is a wonderful thing! If my mind can become even a little more calm, a little more quiet, centered, focused, and one-pointed—oh, this is where happiness lies, this is the way!" We have to keep going, on and on. At some sessions the mind begins to cooperate; everything is much easier and nice and calm. Now we've got it, we think, only to find with the next session that our thoughts are completely all over the place. But it is all right. There is no problem. If the mind wants to be wild and distracted, just let it be wild and distracted, but slowly pull it back—that's the way to go.

Of course the mind has thoughts; it's the nature of the mind to have thoughts. If we think of the mind as like the ocean, then the surface of the ocean has waves. No problem. If we think of the mind as like the sky, then the sky has clouds. So don't worry about the thoughts! Let them go, without giving them any energy. Apart from the fact that the mind has thoughts, there are basically two problems we encounter in our practice. The first one is called drowsiness, or sinking. This means when we sit, we begin to feel very sleepy—that's gross sinking, and very common. When the great eleventh-century Tibetan yogi Milarepa started to meditate, he placed a lighted butter lamp on his head. So he obviously had his problems, too. A friend of mine used a small bowl filled to the brim with water on her head. These are just ways to keep us from not nodding off! We have to be inventive and not give in to drowsiness.

Subtle sinking is more dangerous because it's less obvious. We can get into a state which is calm and peaceful, but with little awareness, and we can sit like that for hours. A genuine meditative mind is very relaxed and spacious but totally alert, very bright and clear. So if we are in a state where we are very calm and spacious but there isn't that vivid clarity or alert awareness, then we are sinking. This is dangerous, as one can stay in that state for a long time and think that one is going into deep meditation. But this is not meditation. It is just a subtle state of sinking, and afterwards, when we come out of meditation, we kind of drift and float around: everything is beautiful and peaceful, the bliss cloud syndrome. Then we are seriously going astray because we should come out from our meditation feeling quite centered and present, aware and awake. Meditation is the process of waking up, not putting ourselves to sleep.

The other main problem of course is our old companion distraction. If the mind is over-active and very distracted, the antidote to that is to be in a slightly warmer room, to wear heavier clothing, to eat more food, and in general to get more grounded. Sometimes we visualize a dark spot just below the navel to bring the mind down. It is said also that we should think of the sufferings of samsara and the fact of impermanence and death and that we don't have time to waste, so that we can sit with a sense of urgency. Since we have wasted so much time already, this is not the time to carry on wasting more. This is the time for meditation. It is the time to be serious and to put all our efforts into doing this practice. We must not just dissipate our energies again by thinking many thoughts, getting very agitated, wanting to get up and go somewhere else. We have to be very strong with ourselves, very firm and clear about what we are going to do.

The important thing we have to do is just bring the quality of knowing, of attention, to the breath. Breathing in, breathing out—just to know it, not to change the breath in any way or comment on it, not to think about it and analyze it, but just to know the breath and experience it in the moment as much as possible. As soon as we are commenting mentally, we are not with the breath; we are just thinking about it again. All the thoughts that come into the mind are traditionally said to be like unwanted guests. They are waiting to be asked to sit down, but nobody asks them to do so. Certainly, we don't offer them tea or ask them how they are. We ignore them. Eventually they get embarrassed, and after a while they leave.

Our attention is only on the breathing in and the breathing out—that's all we have to do. If our mind strays and we get caught up again in thoughts, we just let them go and come back to the breathing. If we spend the whole time being with the breathing, getting lost, bringing the mind back, going off again and bringing the mind back again, that's fine, no problem. Slowly, slowly, our breathing begins to stand out more, becoming more clear and vivid, while other things recede into the background. Thoughts and sounds become just distant rumbles. Eventually, of course, they will begin to quieten down of themselves, but this won't happen immediately. The real qualities needed for the spiritual life are patience and perseverance.

PRAJNA PARAMITA, OR WISDOM

We have looked into shamatha a little bit, this idea of making the mind more quiet and collected, more one-pointed. We have also considered the fact that shamatha helps the mind see to the bottom of the lake. But it doesn't remove the mud; it doesn't remove all the garbage and all the weeds at the bottom.

When I was in Lahaul, outside my cave, there was a flat area sort of like a patio. It was of hardened earth and on the surface were clusters of pretty little flowers. When it rained or snowed, it all got very muddy, and I decided to put down some large flat stones. That meant I had to pull out these small flowers. I decided that the only way to get rid of these delicate flowers was not just to remove them, but to really pull out the whole root system so they wouldn't grow again. I imagined that I could just pull and it would come out. But as I started to trace the roots of these little flowers, I discovered that they literally went all the way across the patio. The roots were spread out and interconnected through a huge underground network, although only a few little clusters of flowers were visible on the surface. The weeds of our mind are like this. On top, they look attractive. "Oh, I love chocolates," or "I love new clothes." So innocent. But these roots of our desire are deep and thick and they spread out and underlie everything. This is the problem. These roots of our negativities, our delusions, our ill-will, and our greed are so deeply imbedded in our mind that they permeate everything, and often we don't even recognize them for what they really are. We may ask, what is the point of pulling them out? We pull out a bit here and we snip and trim a little bit there, but that doesn't deal with the pervasive root system.

It seems to me that vipashyana meditation is dealing with the mind on two fronts that ultimately come together as the realization of the empty nature of the mind. First of all, we are dealing with the fact that our mind is permeated by these very deep negative impulses which create so much pain and problems in our lives, for ourselves and for others around us. Then beyond that, there is the whole question of who experiences this pain and these problems in the first place. So we will deal with these just in brief, as this is a huge subject.

Through the practice of shamatha, our mind quiets down a bit. And as our mind quiets down, our thought stream usually goes through three stages. At first, it is like a waterfall, just crashing and cascading down. And then it becomes like a turbulent river, gradually becoming more placid as it goes along. Eventually, the river opens into the ocean. Perhaps now in our calm-abiding meditation practice our mind has got to the point where it is no longer a cascading waterfall; it is more like a calmly flowing river. At this point, we don't need to go into that ocean of samadhi, or deep absorption. That is not so important here. We just need to get our mind more quiet; we just need to acquire the ability to concentrate on one point, to have single-pointed concentration. These two are required, but we don't need to be in the state with no thoughts whatsoever.

Previously, as we were developing one-pointed concentration, we ignored the thoughts. We didn't give the thoughts any attention. We were giving attention to the focal point of our concentration, which was the breath. Now, however, we apply that concentration to the thoughts themselves. This is said to be like somebody sitting on the bank of a river just watching it go by. We are not trying to dam up the river, or change the river flow in any way; we are just sitting on the banks of our mental river, watching the thoughts flow by. We are not trying to interfere with the thoughts. We are not doing anything about the thoughts. The important thing is not to be fascinated or caught up with the thoughts—"*Oh, that's an interesting idea. Hmm, yeah, right*"—and in the next minute, our mind is swept away downriver. "*That's a terrible thought. How could I think of something like that? I am supposed to be a Dharma student. A Dharma student never thinks like that,*" and again we get swept away. We need to just watch the thoughts flowing by. However, there are some simple dos and don'ts of watching the mind. If we watch the mind very tensely, keeping all the thoughts together, ready to pounce the minute we forget anything or if any thought wanders off—"every thought, mustn't miss a thought"—we end up with what is called in Tibetan *lung* (pronounced "loong"), which is the imbalance of primal energy, or what is called *qi* in Chinese. The Zen teacher Suzuki Roshi said that the way to control your cow is to give it a large pasture. As we try to develop these qualities of awareness and mindfulness and observing the mind, it is very important to give the mind a wide pasture and not keep it too tight. That extreme tenseness is not what we mean. Rather we mean this sense of allowing our thoughts to come and to flow, and meanwhile, we are just knowing, just observing, just seeing the thoughts, and if we miss a few, it doesn't matter.

So this is the next stage after we have been practicing with the breathing or with some object in front of ourselves. When the thoughts have calmed down a little and are not so chaotic, and when our one-pointedness, concentration, and awareness have become a little more strong and well-defined, then we turn the attention from the breathing to the mind itself. According to Buddhist psychology, we cannot have two thought moments at the same time. Two mental states cannot arise in our consciousness simultaneously. Our mental states are incredibly rapid but nevertheless they are sequential. Therefore, as we have more moments of awareness, we have fewer moments of discursive thinking. As our awareness becomes stronger and more constant, it stops jumping back and forth between awareness and discursive moments and becomes just awareness. Thoughts begin to slow down, there are fewer thoughts, until finally it appears that the thoughts have completely stopped. There is no more movement in the mind. The mind is completely quiet and the awareness is extremely sharp. When we get to that point, then we start to develop what is called insight. We begin to use this intelligence to look into the mind itself.

As I said previously, we live from our mind; we only experience anything through our mind. Yet we don't know that mind itself. We've never looked at it. We say, "I think," "I remember," "in my opinion," "my judgment is." We are full of judgments, intentions, ideas, thoughts, fantasies, dreams, and memories, but what is a thought? What does it look like? Where does it come from? Where does it stay? Where does it go? What does it feel like? What does it look like? "I'm angry," "I'm happy," "I'm sad"—but what does an emotion look like? Where is it coming from? So we use the mind to look at the mind. We try to see what a thought is—what does it look like? What is it? We can think about a thought, but can we actually experience a thought?

We can continue to investigate the mind. "Okay, there are times when there are thoughts. And then there are times when there are no thoughts." Is that the same or different? And then what about the awareness which is observing the thoughts—is that awareness the same as the thoughts, or is it different? And what does that awareness look like? Can we see the seer? Can we observe the observer?

And then, of course, we may ask ourselves the question of questions: "Who is the observer?" I am not giving you the answer! We say, "I think," "I remember," "I like," "I do not like," "I am happy," "I am sad," "I am a good person," "I am a bad person," but who is this "I"? Normally we never ask; we never look. This is the heart of it because we are always clinging to our false identifications which cause us so much confusion and misery.

We identify, first of all, with the particular body we have: "I am a woman," "I am a man," "I am white," "I am black," "I am brown," "I am Asian," "I am European," "I am American," "I am African," "I am beautiful," "I am ugly," "I am tall," "I am thin," "I am fat," "this is me." But of course we are not our bodies. We are connected with our bodies, but we are not our bodies. When we die, we leave behind the body, and the consciousness goes on. All those memories, all those identifications which are bound to our physical form are only temporary. They are not who we really are. They are the role we are playing at this particular point.

We have all had endless numbers of lifetimes, in endlessly different forms, certainly as both male and female, in many different countries, in many different guises; and each time we thought, "This is me; this is who I am." When we die, we abandon that particular form, and as we take on a new form we think, "This is me; this is who I am." We identify with our thoughts, our opinions, and our judgments, and we identify with our memories, especially sad ones, especially difficult ones. We cling, and we revolve our whole identity around our suffering. We are such perverse beings, but when we look into our mind, we see that memories are just thoughts—that's all. Events that we are remembering are over; they were gone years ago. They are not here; they do not exist. All that we are left with are our thoughts, but when we look into our thoughts, in themselves they are quite transparent. A thought is not a thing. So why are we are identifying with them so closely?

In one of the sutras, Ananda, who was the Buddha's cousin and attendant, says to him, "How is it that all these other buddhas have beautiful pure buddha realms where it is so perfect and lovely, and you have such an awful buddha realm?"

And the Buddha said, "My buddha realm is completely perfect. It is just your impure mind which sees it as awful."

Our impure perceptions create the reality we perceive. But of course that is not to say that therefore the whole of external phenomena is purely illusion. It is not exactly an illusion. The Tibetans say it is like an illusion. It is like an illusion because we project and are not conscious that this is our projection. Since our perceptions are ego-distorted and impure, we do not see things as they really are. We only perceive our own version, which is based on delusion.

We are looking at the mind. We are looking at the flow of thoughts. Now, while we are observing the thoughts, and the awareness is very strong, the thoughts begin to slow down. It is like a film: if the film begins to go slower and slower, then one recognizes the individual frames rather than the projected movie. Likewise, if our awareness is clear and steady, the thoughts begin to slow down and can be recognized as thoughts linked together. And it can happen that when our awareness is very clear, the stream of thoughts parts for a moment, and there is a gap between the last thought and the next. When there is a gap, the observer directly merges with that which is underlying the thought, the clear light nature of the mind. In that moment there is the direct intuition and realization of the nature of the mind: non-dual, non-conceptual, unconditioned, beyond thought. We can't think about it, but we can experience it.

In this kind of meditation the idea is to get as many flashes as we can of these moments of non-dual vision and to prolong them. As the mind naturally rests in this unborn awareness ever more frequently and for longer periods, eventually the meditator will remain in that state of wakefulness the whole time. It is a level of awareness which has no boundaries. There is no self and other. The sky has no center and the sky has no circumference; it is boundless. Now the sky is all-pervading, not just above us but everywhere. It is space. Without space, we could not have anything because space is everything. Everything comprises space with just a few protons and neutrons swirling around. If there were no space, nothing could exist.

When we come into this room we see the people, we see the chairs, we see the microphone on the table, but we can only see them because of space. And yet we don't see space itself. Outside, inside: it is all space. I read somewhere that the actual solid mass of the human body occupies a space no bigger than the head of a pin. It is all space, and that spaciousness is reflected in the true nature of the mind. When we talk of our true self, we have the idea of someone sitting inside us—a bigger, better, more wonderful *me*. But that is not what we are talking about at all. When we realize the true nature of our being, where is "I," where is "other"? In space, I can't say that this is my bit of space, and that is your bit of space. It is just space. Where is the boundary? On the earth we can put up fences, but in space how can you put up fences? Where does it begin? Where does it end? And the true nature of the mind is like that.

The true nature of mind is beginningless and endless and it has no center and no circumference. It is a boundless interconnection with all beings. It cannot be seen; it cannot be thought about conceptually. But it certainly can be experienced and realized. It is the mind of a buddha. And this vast, spacious quality of the mind is filled with all the wonderful qualities of wisdom and compassion and purity. It is not empty or vacuous. Comparing the nature of mind to the sky is good because it gives us a vast feeling of infinity. But space isn't conscious, whereas the essential quality of this inner spaciousness is awareness, knowing. If we did not have this quality of knowing, we could not exist. It is clear awareness behind the working of our senses that allows us to know anything; it illumines our thinking and our emotions. Behind the movement of the conceptual mind is vast silent knowing. It is so simple. But we don't believe it. And it is sad indeed that we miss it. We overlook the simplicity in front of us.

When I was about seventeen or eighteen, I worked in a library. At that time, my mind changed for a while. I was very conscious that when sounds came into my ears, they were merely vibrations hitting on my eardrums; and I was very conscious that the things I saw were just things that were being seen. My mind was as an empty house in which all the doors and windows were open and the winds were blowing through and no one was at home. I was very aware of each of the senses, each working in its own sphere, but they were not me or mine. Now this may sound very cold, but in fact as I looked into the eyes of the other people around me, I could see how extremely involved they were in what they heard and saw and thought, and how there was no inner space. On account of this their minds were so turbulent, just as my own mind normally was. Immense compassion arose within me because I understood our predicament so clearly.

Genuine compassion arises from insight. Normally when we look and when we experience anything, we really believe in what we are seeing and experiencing. We are completely involved. It is as if there is no space inside. But when we develop pure awareness then we are not submerged by our thoughts. Awareness is always behind the thoughts and feelings.

And so we practice. We practice being able to stand back to see the thoughts, memories, feelings, and emotions as merely thoughts, memories, and feelings, as merely mental states, and not something solid or real. "Me" and "mine" are just mental states. Mental states come; they stay for a moment; and they go. That's all that is actually happening, but because we have no space in our mind, we can't see that. Meditation allows us to have the room to see that our thoughts and our feelings are not something solid, not something opaque. They are empty in their nature, like a bubble. We cannot catch hold of them. If we look into the thought itself, it evaporates. Ultimately, this is the most skillful way to deal with emotions because then as any emotion comes up, we can look directly into it, and in that moment of seeing, it just disappears. Take a negative emotion like anger as an example. In the very moment that the angry thought is incipient within us, if there is recognition, then that anger spontaneously transforms into a subtle form of energy which is very clear and sharp. These poisons of the mind, if taken to their very roots, are a source of great wisdom energy. The problem is that we allow them to develop unrecognized and they emerge in very distorted forms such as greed, anger, and jealousy. But if we can catch them right at that moment when they are emerging into consciousness then they have a vibrancy and a clarity. It is an extremely clear form of energy.

It is said in the higher teachings that the greater our emotional defilements, the greater our wisdom. But until we can catch the thought in its incipient form, in its moment of being born—unless we can do that and transform it in that instant—then of course it is better to try to deal with negative emotions in other ways. But once we can do that, once we have that extremely powerful awareness which sees things very clearly moment to moment to moment, then there is nothing to fear because every thought that turns up is transformed into wisdom energy.

As it says in the Tibetan texts, "Look, where is the mind? Is it in the stomach? Is it in the foot? Is it in the heart? Is it in the shoulder?" They seem never to ask in these texts, "Is it in the head?" Isn't that interesting? Perhaps it never occurred to them that it is possible for the mind to be in the head. At one time, I remember my lama, Khamtrul Rinpoche, saying how curious it was that Westerners think that the mind is in the head. He said the brain is in the head, but the brain isn't the mind. Not long ago, I was reading a book by a famous brain surgeon, who said, "We now know a lot about the brain but we still haven't found the mind." The brain is the computer, but it is not the energy running the computer. When Westerners, who are very head-oriented, meditate, it often happens that meditation stays up in the head. Sometimes people get headaches because of it.

If someone said to me, "I know this morning you came in and you stole my wallet. You are a thief!" I would say, "You mean me?" and point to my chest. I wouldn't say, "You mean me?" and point to my head. Now why not? Our senses are in our head—our eyes, our ears, our nose, our mouth. So why don't we point at our head as we say "me"?

When we begin to meditate, there is oneself, the subject, and there is the object of meditation. Someone described it as two mountains facing each other, and that is why meditation remains a matter of the intellect. It is still part of our thoughts. Now when the meditation begins to deepen and the subject and object begin to merge, when I am no longer meditating—when I am the meditation—then the focus comes into the heart. When the meditation is in the heart, there is no duality between subject and object. They merge; we become the meditation. Meditation brings our practice from the head to the heart.

Although in the beginning it usually does not happen, it is very important that we try somehow to draw the meditation down into the heart center. It is for this reason that many of the tantric meditations are centered on the heart chakra. For Westerners especially, and Asians who have been educated in Western situations, we are already too much up in our heads. When we meditate, we turn it into another intellectual exercise and it doesn't really transform us. Often during our retreat time our thoughts calm down; we become peaceful and centered. But when we go out into the world, it all falls apart again! And that is because we haven't become one with the meditation. Inner transformation can only take place when the arena of action is shifted down to the heart chakra. Otherwise, there is always a separation. I want to emphasize that because it is an important point. Some people have been meditating for years and years but it is still up in the head. Nothing much has changed and they feel discouraged.

The perfection of wisdom has to do with this quality of emptiness. Now Buddhists talk about emptiness a lot. I am not a philosopher, so I am not going to give you a discourse on Madhyamika. But when Buddhists say that everything is empty, they are basically talking about two things: one is that nothing exists from its own side; nothing exists in and of itself. Everything can only appear in relationship with everything else. It's fairly obvious. We cannot think about dark unless we think about light. We cannot have left unless we have right. We cannot think except in relative terms. Western phi-losophy deals with this, too. There are scholars in the Buddhist tradition who analyze everything down to its component parts. Take the watch. If I say to you, "What is this?" You will reply, "This is a watch." Then we can question, "Which part of it is the watch? Is it the front? Is it the back? Is it the hands? Is it the inside machinery?" We keep inquiring to find the "watchness" of the watch, but we can never the find the watch in itself. It is only a label which we give to a combination of many, many things. The thing in itself doesn't exist. It is empty of self-existence. We can never ever find the thing in and of itself. Everything that we see and experience is just a conventional label. People spend thirty years studying this approach. You are lucky—you got it in just a few sentences!

The other meaning of emptiness is what we addressed earlier—this spa-cious quality of everything which allows itself to be filled, but that which fills it is itself empty. And this applies also to the mind. Philosophers and scholars spend many years analyzing external reality. Yogis analyze internal reality.

During my first meditation lesson from my old yogi teacher, he pointed to a small table and asked, "Is that table empty?"

"Yes," I said. I had done my Buddhist studies.

"Do you see it as empty?"

"No," I replied.

"Your mind," he said. "Is your mind empty?"

"Yes," I said, with a bit more confidence.

"Do you see it as empty?"

"No."

"Which do you think would be easier, to see the table as empty, or to see your mind as empty?" the old yogi asked.

"Oh, definitely, to see the mind as empty," I said.

He laughed and said, "Okay, then you can stay with us!"

Naturally I had a question of my own. "Well, if I had said that seeing the emptiness of the table was easier, what would you have done?"

"Then I would have told you to go down to Sera Monastery," the yogi replied. Sera Monastery is a big monastic college where they study and debate topics such as the emptiness of the table.

But in the yogic tradition we study the emptiness of the mind because once we understand the emptiness of the mind, then we understand everything. When we realize the nature of mind, we do not just think about it but rather see directly how the mind works, and how it projects external reality.

Consider how any physicist will tell you that this table is basically empty. It is basically space with just a few protons and neutrons whizzing around. But we don't see it like that. We don't experience it like that. We experience the table as something very solid. It would be heavy for me to lift. While that may be how I would experience it, that is not how a physicist would see the matter, is it? So what I am experiencing is what my mind projects. Now if I were to have very different senses and a different kind of mind, I would probably experience this table in a completely different way. If I was one of those little worms that bore into wood, I would apprehend this in a very dissimilar manner, but that would also be real. It would be real to a woodworm.

We believe what our senses tell us, but then there are also phenomena which directly contradict our understanding of the world. For instance, there are enlightened masters who leave their handprints and footprints in solid rock. We can see them. Even the present Karmapa as a boy left his handprints and footprints all over rocks near his monastery in Tibet before he left for India. Now how could he do that? He could do that because his mind, being more tuned into reality than our own, saw that the rock is not as solid as it looks. But we believe our senses, and we have a kind of consensus and conspiracy to see things the way our sense perceptions present them. This is fine because this is how we function, and there is nothing wrong with it on a relative level. This is how we are equipped to deal with life on a conventional plane. But the problem arises when we think that it is true. The problem comes because we trust that our conditioned thoughts are telling us the truth.

We believe implicitly in our very transient identities. The problem is not the ego—the problem is our identification with the ego. The solution is to know that we are just playing a role, like an actor. In order to be convincing, the actor has to play the part as persuasively as possible. An actor identifies with the role. But what big trouble if this actor comes off the stage and still thinks that the role is who he or she is! The term "personality" comes from the Latin word *persona*, which was the mask worn on stage by actors to represent the different characters. Our problem is that we never take off our masks even in the privacy of our own bedroom. We think, "This is who I really am."

In tantric meditations, one sees oneself as a deity. For example, one sees oneself as Chenrezig, the Bodhisattva of Compassion. However when people are doing the meditation, especially foreigners (and maybe even Tibetans), we sit there visualizing ourselves: white, with four arms, and radiating light. But the inner thought is "I am Mary Smith and now I am pretending to be Chenrezig." And we think that this is the reality. We think that that's the truth. But of course the real truth is that we are actually Chenrezig pretending to be Mary Smith! This basic delusion—that we identify with the wrong things—is at the root of all our problems.

When we become enlightened, we don't become some kind of cosmic blob, spaced out in space awareness. It is not like that. If you have ever met any great enlightened masters, you realize that they are more vital, more completely present, more vivid than ordinary people. They know who they are and who they are not. They are conscious of this present form they embody, but it is just their present form. It is not who and what they are.

Behind all that we identify with is the vast open spacious awareness which is not only knowing but is in itself the fullness of complete wisdom and compassion. Wisdom means that we see things as they really are. We understand things clearly, without distortions. When we are looking at wisdom and emptiness, it is not at something that is cold and remote. This open spacious awareness contains everything.

The Buddha's mind is empty, and because it is empty it can be full of all the Buddha's qualities. We are full of all the Buddha's qualities. We have just covered them over for the moment in our forgetfulness. The only way to discover them is to look inside and begin to strip away the false veils, the veils which cover what is always present and waiting to be found.

✐ QUESTIONS

Q: How can we help our children to access the benefit of stillness?

JTP: Once, when I was going on a bus to Dharamsala, I sat next to a young man who turned out to be a kindergarten teacher in New York at a school that was influenced by Krishnamurti. They taught all their children how to sit and focus on the breathing and on the mind. He said it was brilliant! The children loved it; they naturally accessed it. They were told what to do and they did it quite easily because children's minds are very open. It helped them a lot to become centered, to realize that there *is* a center. Teaching them how to access their quiet inner center is terribly important.

I also met someone who was dealing with disturbed children, children whose behavior was so extreme that they couldn't be handled any more. One of the many things they did was to teach them just to learn how to sit and how to begin learning to find their own calm center. I think that is one of the greatest gifts we can give a child. Of course, especially with very young children, one has to be skillful and not keep things too long, since nowadays the attention span of children is so short. We can make it almost like play— nothing really ponderous—we're just helping children learn how to sit and come into their center, even for a few minutes. If you are a religious family, you can come together when the children wake up and when they go to bed. If you have a little shrine, you can light incense and candles together, say a little prayer, and spend special time together to become centered before falling asleep. It would be wonderful.

In the old days, families always came together in the evenings and said their family prayers. It is really very sad that we have lost some of these intelligent traditions. If we are serious about our children's welfare, we should in a very gentle way begin to introduce such things. It seems to me that moments which the family share together are very precious, especially things which help the children to become grounded and calm and feel that sense of security. Perhaps it is something missing nowadays from many families.

Q: I am wondering if you can talk a bit about meditation and sleeping and the relationship to dreaming. Sometimes when I meditate, I either get into the sleeping sort of sinking state or I get so wide awake that I can't go to sleep.

JTP: The Tibetans, who never like to waste a minute, have two main practices for sleep. One is called the clear light meditation and one is called dream yoga. However, I am not going to teach you about that. The answer is always to get the balance so that our awareness is there and we can maintain that awareness into our dream state, but we must not be so aware that we don't go to sleep at all. If we are meditating but we feel sleepy and can't keep awake, then we are sinking into drowsiness. We tend either to just get more sleepy, and that is not good because it sets the pattern in the mind that meditation is falling asleep, or we wake ourselves up and we can't sleep at all. So it is a little better to do our main meditation some time before we go to sleep. Then when we are going to sleep, we keep our basic awareness present, but low key; we just relax and practice letting the mind go, letting all thoughts go, not holding on to anything except the awareness. That is a quick way to put ourselves to sleep but at the same time maintain a spark of awareness through it all. Then when we fall asleep, our dreams will also be quite clear and we can recognize them as dreams. We will wake up in a state of clarity and awareness. This is one of the reasons why Tibetans in retreats like to sit up and not lie down to sleep because then it's much easier to maintain awareness. Once we lie down, our awareness tends to spread out, and then it blanks out altogether. It is an art to carry on enough so that we still have the awareness there, but not so much that we can't sleep at all. Practice!

Q: Sometimes, I find that I am much more awake and alive if I meditate at night instead of sleep. Can I do this?

JTP: Sure, if the next day you are not overly tired. If we are meditating, our mind is relaxed but alert, and actually that is a much more relaxing state of mind than most people's dream state. Our mind is refreshed at very deep levels, but we have to be sure what our body is feeling. So if our mind is feeling very bright and spacious but our body is tired, then we should be cautious. People in retreat usually find that their sleeping time gets less and less. Sometimes, although they are meditating twenty-four hours a day for days on end, they end up feeling more alive and awake. During sleep we are often tossing and turning with endless dreams churning in the mind. That is much more exhausting. It is wonderful to meditate at night when it is so quiet and the world seems suspended, just as long as the body and mind are not affected adversely by fatigue later. It's a very different experience to meditate at night than during the day.

Q: I'd like to ask you about headaches. Sometimes during meditation I feel like if I get too high, I get a bit of a pain, and if I shift my focus, the pain goes up. So I am wondering if that is something to avoid or something to just feel as a sensation.

JTP: What are you are meditating on?

Q: Just looking within and the breath.

JTP: How long has this been happening?

Q: Two months.

JTP: And does it happen every time you meditate on the breath, or only sometimes?

Q: Only sometimes.

JTP: The thing is that when we are meditating, sometimes we try to concentrate too hard and this brings stress to the brain. So it's very important that when we concentrate we also have a mind that stays very relaxed. I cannot express to you how important it is to have a relaxed, and not a tense, mind. I think it is the tension that is giving you the headaches. While sitting and focusing on the ingoing and outgoing of the breath, do it in a way that is very spacious, very soft, and just ignore the rest of what is going on; try not to think about it. Just concentrate by gently bringing the attention to the breathing in and breathing out in a very relaxed way. At the same time, focus very clearly. It's not like forcing yourself to do anything. There is no tension.

The Buddha said that meditation is like tuning guitar strings. If we tune them too tightly, they can snap. And if we tune too softly, we don't get any sound. We have to learn how to tune our instrument to get the beautiful sound. So when we are meditating, we have to work with our mind to get this balance of open relaxation and precise awareness. If you feel that your mind is tense and you are getting headaches, just relax and very gently bring your attention back to the breathing in and breathing out. Maybe shorten the time you are sitting. How long do you sit?

Q: About an hour.

JTP: Maybe that is too long. Do twenty minutes, relax for ten minutes, and do another twenty minutes.

Q: I think some of the tension comes from wondering where to put meditation in the day—to maintain the discipline of continuing the practice, yet also be relaxed and at ease.

JTP: Yes, don't push too hard. During the day, if you can, bring your attention back to the moment. It should not be a harsh discipline for the mind. Practice should be a cause of joy. If we consider our everyday life and our ordinary mind as a big lump of dough, then the practice of awareness is like the yeast. If we mix that with the dough, it lightens it up so that we can cook it and eat it. It's not like having a big ball of uncooked dough in our tummy. It's nourishing because of the yeast. So practice should be like yeast. It shouldn't be like adding a pile of gravel so that our life becomes even more heavy.

Q: Perhaps I should retrain my horse a little bit.

JTP: Yes, be nice to your horse. Stroke him!

Q: I have a question about the breath: do we breathe through the nose or the mouth? I don't understand the difference.

JTP: The Tibetans usually breathe through the nose. It's a very simple thing: breathing in and breathing out. Here we are not particularly focusing on the breath just below the nostrils; it's just a general knowing of the breath coming in and the breath going out. But if it helps the concentration to become more clear then we can localize it. Or we can concentrate at a point just below the navel. We can feel the breath coming in and out. On the other hand, some people have problems with their breath. They get anxious. They get anxiety attacks. In that case, it might be better to use a different object of meditation.

Q: I'd like to ask a question about the gaze because I used to meditate with my eyes closed. Recently I learned to meditate with my eyes open, and I found two things: if I start to fall into that sluggish state, I lift my gaze. I just don't quite understand the quality of the gaze. Sometimes I sort of blur my gaze, as I get distracted by what is in front of me.

JTP: The reason why the Tibetans, Japanese, and Chinese emphasized the gaze with eyes open is because of the connection between the eye organ and the subtle energies of the body. If the gaze is unwavering, it helps the subtle energies to enter into the central channel, which then means the mind quickly becomes one-pointed and calm.

When I first started to meditate, my old yogi teacher handed me a small pebble and I had to put it in front of me and concentrate on it. They suggest a pebble because one cannot be too fascinated by the object; there cannot be too many ideas about it. If the object is a crystal, then we sit there thinking about crystals, and so on. A pebble is a pebble. And as a pebble doesn't reflect light, it doesn't hurt the eyes. It is just there. The idea is to first learn how to focus the gaze and thus learn how to focus the mind. To keep the mind one-pointed on the pebble is quite an achievement, and so that is good training. We don't stare at it. We kind of unfocus our eyes a bit, but keep looking at one point. At first it's a strain for the eyes: they start to water, and so then we close them and open them again.

If we meditate with closed eyes, there is a subtle darkness in the mind. We can become a bit too disconnected with the outside environment. Keeping our eyes open a little, not wide open but slightly, keeps us grounded and that is very important in Buddhist meditation. Initially, it is more difficult than keeping the eyes closed, but in the end, the rewards are great. So you should keep practicing that. Get yourself a little pebble, and go for it!

7

Lojong and Bodhichitta

PUTTING OTHERS before ourselves is an attitude that in Mahayana Buddhism is called mind training, or *lojong* in Tibetan. As we learn to generate great compassion and become clear in our motivation regarding others and ourselves, we deepen our spiritual practice. Lojong is a means for opening ourselves to life.

Buddhist practitioners may be said to comprise those who practice the path for personal liberation and those who practice for universal liberation. Even in the Theravada tradition as recorded in the Pali canon, the Buddha elucidated these two paths—the path of individual liberation achieved by an arhat, and the bodhisattva path which leads to complete enlightenment. The Buddha himself relates how in a past life, when he was still a bodhisattva, he made the profound decision to renounce immediate nirvana as an arhat in order to carry on for many more aeons and become a Buddha out of compassion for the world.

After the Buddha entered into Mahaparinirvana, a Buddhist council was convened with five hundred arhats. The basic canon was recited, and the arhats agreed on what would be included. Now even at that time, as is reported in the canon, a group of monks called the Maha Sangha, or the great community, said at the end of the recitation, "Well, that's very fine, and you've recited it very nicely, but we didn't hear it that way. That's not what we heard the Buddha say, so you can go ahead with your version and we will keep ours. Thank you." And they left. Interestingly, we don't know who these people actually were. What did they hear? Their version seems to have died out, unless it was incorporated into later traditions.

After the Buddha's Mahaparinirvana, monks set out in all directions across India, and within a relatively short time, what are called the eighteen schools developed. These schools maintained their sutras in different languages. It should be understood that the Buddha probably didn't speak Pali, which I think was a West Indian dialect. Historians think that the Buddha probably spoke Prakrit, but in any case most of the different lineages kept their sutras in Sanskrit which was the literary language of the day. But for three hundred years nobody wrote down the canon. It was all memorized and passed on orally.

It happened that the great Emperor Ashoka followed in particular the teachings of the Pali canon, in the school of the Theravada, and so when his son, who was a monk arhat, was sent to Sri Lanka, this school was transmitted there. Eventually it spread out through Thailand, Burma, Cambodia, Laos, and so forth. Later on, when Buddhism more or less died out in India, the only lineages among those eighteen schools still left in the world were the Theravada and those lineages carried and preserved in East Asia, such as in China and Tibet.

On a deep level, the main concern in Buddhism is how to gain liberation. This means that whichever Buddhist country we travel to, we find that behind the basic ethical and social protocol of being a Buddhist there is the understanding that our minds are deluded and need to be liberated. It is as if we are sinking in the swamp of samsara. Our real reason then for having a human life is to rescue ourselves and get out onto dry land. But surely, just from an ordinary point of view, if we do get out onto dry land, our next action would be to turn and pull out all the others. The only point in being on dry land is to be in a position to rescue everyone else. This is the main divide between the so-called Hinayana schools and the Mahayana schools, the *motivation* for liberation. Do we want to be free in order just to be free ourselves? Or do we want to be free so that we are in a position to free others? That is really the big difference.

Being a Buddhist is not a matter of particular practices or robes or what we outwardly call ourselves. We can do vipassana practices wearing a Theravadin robe, but with a bodhisattva motivation, and be on a Mahayana path. We can practice the highest tantras, and if our real motivation is to just liberate ourselves or gain power for ourselves, then we are on a Hinayana path. Hinayana does not have anything to do with Theravada per se: it has to do with our motivation as to why we practice. I know a number of Theravadin monks and nuns who have taken the bodhisattva vow, and even some Catholic monks and nuns who have taken the vow as well. They don't stop being

Theravadin; they don't stop being Catholic. It has nothing to do with that. Spiritual practice has everything to do with our inner motivation.

We have been born endlessly in samsara millions of times and in all realms of existence. We have been born not only as humans but as animals, insects, gods, beings in the hell realms, ghosts, or as anything we can imagine. We have all gone through it over and over, and through all these countless lives we have been interconnected with all beings.

All beings at some time have been our mother; therefore, we have a very deep and close connection with every sentient being. But we have forgotten this. When we meet others now, they look like strangers. And yet just as we wish to care for and liberate our mother in this present lifetime, so can we likewise extend our wish to include all beings. Naturally then the question arises: what is the best and most lasting way that we can be of benefit to our mother, and not just for this lifetime but through endless lifetimes? Clearly the best way to be of help is to see to it that one's mother attains liberation from the endless round of birth and death. We can see to it that she is finally safe and on dry land. But how can we liberate others when we ourselves are still trapped in samsara? We vow, therefore, to attain enlightenment for the sake of all our mother sentient beings.

Our whole attitude toward life is altered when we open ourselves to the bodhisattva vow. It means that our spiritual progress unfolds for the sake of others. Yes, we benefit ourselves, but the ultimate intent is to prepare ourselves so that we can really be of benefit to others. Suppose we are sick and decide that the best way to heal ourselves is to become a doctor. But as we learn the necessary skills, we may realize that there are so many others who are also sick. Naturally, it makes more sense to train to become a doctor not just so we can heal ourselves but so we can heal others, too.

Sentient beings are infinite in number. *Beings* doesn't mean just human beings but also animals and insects and beings in the spirit realms. There are so many beings, and in one lifetime it is not possible to liberate them all. Even the Buddha could not accomplish that. But we have endless lifetimes, and so we go for refuge, not until our present life ends but until enlightenment is reached and all sentient beings have been liberated. That is a long time. As bodhisattvas on the path, this attitude pervades everything we do, every meditation and all our prayers and service during our daily life. The ultimate aim is to spiritually advance and be able to genuinely benefit others. A very simple example comes to mind. I used to do a certain spiritual practice, and one evening I was feeling tired, and decided I wouldn't bother to do it. But then I thought, "No, wait a minute. You're not doing this for your sake. You're a representative, the substitute for all the beings in the world who don't know how to do this practice. You're doing it on their behalf! So what are you saying, you don't feel like it tonight, you're a bit tired?" Immediately the whole situation changed and the energy to continue began to flow. Cherishing others is powerful motivation.

One of our main problems is that we put ourselves first. Even people who are usually very selfless still find that there is a sense of self which they are somehow protecting. If the *Eight Verses of Mind Training* seem extreme, it is because they deal with how we can consider others as being more precious than ourselves. This is why we are going to contemplate them and inquire into their meaning. They reveal how we can wear away our resistance to selflessness. Even feeling resistance to the thought of coming back endlessly into samsara out of compassion is a sign of strong self-cherishing. These eight verses offer methods to help us open to great compassion. Dedicating one's life to serving others is very rare in this world. The bodhisattva vow takes this commitment a step further, transforming it into a genuine spiritual path that extends not just for this lifetime but for endless lifetimes.

Atisha Dipamkara, a great Indian pandita, left for Sumatra to study for years with the great master Dharmamati in order to understand this whole topic of bodhichitta, the aspiring mind that seeks enlightenment for the sake of others. Later, he went to Tibet and introduced the practice of mind training. He also started the Kadampa tradition. The text we will explore here, the *Eight Verses of Mind Training*, was written by Geshe Langri Thangpa, who lived in Tibet from the latter part of the eleventh century into the twelfth century.

EIGHT VERSES OF MIND TRAINING[1]

May I always cherish all beings
With the resolve to accomplish for them
The highest good that is more precious
Than any wish-fulfilling jewel.

1. Translated by Ruth Sonam in *Eight Verses for Training the Mind* by Geshe Sonam Rinchen, translated and edited by Ruth Sonam (Ithaca, NY: Snow Lion Publications, 2001). Reprinted by permission.

Whenever I am in the company of others,
May I regard myself as inferior to all
And from the depths of my heart
Cherish others as supreme.

In all my actions may I watch my mind,
And as soon as disturbing emotions arise,
May I forcefully stop them at once,
Since they will hurt both me and others.

When I see ill-natured people,
Overwhelmed by wrong deeds and pain,
May I cherish them as something rare,
As though I had found a treasure-trove.

When someone out of envy does me wrong
By insulting me and the like,
May I accept defeat
And offer the victory to them.

Even if someone whom I have helped
And in whom I have placed my hopes
Does great wrong by harming me,
May I see them as an excellent spiritual friend.

In brief, directly or indirectly,
May I give all help and joy to my mothers,
And may I take all their harm and pain
Secretly upon myself.

May none of this ever be sullied
By thoughts of the eight worldly concerns.
May I see all things as illusions
And, without attachment, gain freedom from bondage.

This matter of training our mind so that we place others before ourselves underlies the whole of Tibetan Buddhism. For example, my own lama, the

Eighth Khamtrul Rinpoche, was very quiet. When he was a young monk in Tibet he almost never spoke, and even in India he didn't say much. He hardly ever gave any teachings. We learned through his example, by how he acted and not really by what he said. But when he gave the bodhisattva vow he would speak about bodhichitta and Mahayana mind training. He would just talk and talk and get so excited. Words would pour out of him, sometimes for hours. Khamtrul Rinpoche was so enthused by this idea of dedicating one's whole life to the service of others and seeking enlightenment for their sake! He found it deeply inspiring.

We have yogis in our community. They are monks, but until they left Tibet for India, they lived in caves. They do the most advanced tantric practices. Before he died, Khamtrul Rinpoche called the yogis together and said, "Now I am going to give you the supreme secret teaching. This is something from my heart that I have to transmit to you." The yogis all felt very intrigued, wondering what this teaching was going to be. And it turned out to be the lojong text called *Seven Point Mind Training* written in the twelfth century by Chekawa Yeshe Dorje, who was inspired to compose that text by these same *Eight Verses* we are reading now. So lojong teachings are not only given at the beginning of one's practice. They are also given in the middle and at the end. If we could just practice this, that would be enough. We don't need anything more. In all the traditions of Tibet, this is the essence.

His Holiness the Dalai Lama and all the great masters teach these basic principles again and again, because our self-cherishing mind is so strong and so subtle at the same time. This teaching just keeps wearing it away. When non-practitioners think of Tibetan Buddhism, they often think of all the rituals and deities, all the glamour. But when I think of what Tibetan Buddhism is fundamentally about, it is bodhichitta and lojong, which put others before oneself. This is why Tibetan Buddhism has stayed so pure. It hasn't degenerated. Actually tantra came to Thailand, Sri Lanka, and other countries, but after some time it became corrupt. It did not degenerate in Tibet because they have had this incredible emphasis on the purification of motivation from the very beginning.

This quality of bodhichitta is really the essence of the path in Mahayana Buddhism. Books are written praising bodhichitta in beautiful words: how this aspiration for enlightenment for the sake of others really is the wish-fulfilling gem, the jewel beyond price. Tibetans regard bodhichitta as the one practice which completely transforms the whole of our spiritual and worldly life. Awakening to bodhichitta is like changing base metal into gold, and so it is precious beyond words.

The *Eight Verses of Mind Training* challenges what is called the self-cherishing aspect of the mind. It is not intended that we should constantly humiliate and hate ourselves. It does not mean that we should only think about the bad things in ourselves, and that at any time when we think of our good qualities we feel guilty, as though we are being prideful. That way, we end up feeling tight and low in self-esteem.

His Holiness the Dalai Lama is very impressed with science, and every year he holds a mind-science conference that gathers different kinds of top scientists to discuss the similarities and differences between science and Buddhism. His Holiness once had a seminar with all sorts of psychiatrists and neurologists and Western experts concerned with the mind. Perhaps he had been giving some reflections on self-cherishing because one of these scientists asked him, "Well, Your Holiness, how do we deal with low self-esteem and self-hatred?"

His Holiness looked completely blank, and said, "Ah, what do you mean?"

The scientist said, "Well, you know, when you feel unworthy, and you don't like yourself, and you feel very heavy and sad."

His Holiness looked puzzled and asked his translator, "Hmm, what does he mean?" So the translator explained, and His Holiness sat there thinking. He said, "Oh, I think very rare, very rare."

The scientist turned to his eminent colleagues and said, "Who ever suffers from a sense of low self-esteem or self-hatred?"

Everybody put their hands up.

His Holiness had to really think about it because Tibetans, at least traditional Tibetans living in old Tibet, didn't suffer from this. Nowadays, modern young Tibetan refugees have identity problems, but not so much the older ones. They have a great sense of self-worth and self-esteem no matter what their social status. It is not pride. It is a sense of inner confidence, a sense of being basically all right.

Tibetans arriving in India had lost everything. The Chinese Communists had taken over their country. Many Tibetans lost family members and friends who were killed or imprisoned. The Communists destroyed monasteries. They killed monks and nuns and ravaged the culture. They tried to take away that which was most important of all to the Tibetans, which was their

Dharma. Those who were able fled to India and Nepal. Often there were hundreds in a group trying to escape and maybe two or three managed to get out. It took months for the Tibetans to cross over the difficult terrain of the snow-covered mountains. And if they managed it, they found themselves in a completely different culture—the language was different, the food was different, and it was very hot. They were sick and devastated refugees, and they had nothing.

When I first went to India in 1964, the Tibetans had been out for about four years. They were so poor, and many were just living in tents made out of sacks. They were working on the roads, even the lamas. And they were so worried about what was happening to those they had left behind in Tibet. Nonetheless, what struck everybody who met these Tibetan refugees was how cheerful they were! They had such presence. They were so friendly and generous. They weren't self-pitying—they were beautiful, and radiantly at peace with themselves despite the trauma they had suffered.

Exchanging self for others does not leave us feeling depressed and downtrodden and full of self-contempt. In fact it gives us a tremendous sense of inner courage which we can carry with us into even the most disastrous situations.

In the *Bodhicharyavatara (The Way of the Bodhisattva)*, Shantideva points to the difference between ordinary pride and self-confidence. Pride is a klesha, an afflictive emotion, but self-confidence is essential for the spiritual path. Cherishing others beyond ourselves requires an enormous amount of self-confidence and fearlessness. *The Way of the Bodhisattva* and the *Eight Verses of Mind Training* hit at our pride and the tight knot of self-cherishing which seems to sit at the center of our being.

> May I always cherish all beings
> With the resolve to accomplish for them
> The highest good that is more precious
> Than any wish-fulfilling jewel.

The first verse means exactly what it says: May I always hold everyone dear, with the determination to win for them "the highest good," which of course is liberation. All beings without exception want to be happy. They don't want to suffer. As human beings, we expend enormous energy, time, and money on what we hope will make us happy. One of the tragedies of our modern consumer society is that it tries to sell us a deal for happiness which the Buddha already proclaimed as the path to suffering.

Our consumer society is firmly based on the three poisons of greed, hatred, and delusion, with an emphasis on the ever-increasing generation of greed and desire. Our society is founded on self-advertisement, on the selling and promotion of self, and this expression of the three poisons just creates samsara. Our society also glorifies violence. I am always horrified when I get glimpses of the movies people watch in the planes and so on. These movies are full of people fighting and blowing each other up!

So this verse offers us another way of looking at life. As Shantideva says, when we seek only our own happiness, we just end up with more frustration and suffering. But when we seek the happiness of others, we discover our own happiness. Numerically, as sentient beings are infinite and I am just one, it makes more sense to be concerned with the many. His Holiness the Dalai Lama says his first thought on waking in the morning is how he can use this day to bring happiness to others.

In Indian mythology wish-fulfilling jewels belong to the gods, and such jewels grant anything one may wish. And yet the verse tells us that the aspiration to give joy to others beyond ourselves is more precious than such a jewel. The reasoning is that even if we had the wish-fulfilling jewel in our hands, it could only fulfill our wishes in this lifetime. But we will carry with us the aspiration for the happiness and enlightenment of others throughout endless lifetimes, and it will bring us much good karma and benefit. Such aspiration reflects a transformation of the mind, and we will take it with us until enlightenment is reached.

Therefore, the second verse says:

> Whenever I am in the company of others,
> May I regard myself as inferior to all
> And from the depths of my heart
> Cherish others as supreme.

Now I can well understand how certain women might resent this verse and think that as women we have always seen ourselves as inferior. So again I want to emphasize what I said at the beginning. The verse does not suggest that we see ourselves as inferior and others as superior, and that we must be passive and groveling and full of self-contempt. Rather, it is this attitude of delight in bringing happiness to others that is underscored. It is not a matter of subservience but of seeing through our inherent self-concern.

The Buddha spoke of the quality of loving-kindness as being like a mother's love for her only child. And nature programs a mother to love. If nature didn't predispose us to love our little baby, then we might just throw it away because it is too much trouble! But even most animals love their offspring and defend them literally to the death if need be. So we already have that instinct inside us: we just need to promote and expand our natural impulse until that feeling of melting love extends to all beings. Throughout countless lifetimes all beings have been our children and we have been their mother. And they have each been our mother, too. Giving compassion toward all beings completely transforms the heart. It is how we may recognize that every being who comes into our presence wants happiness. Whether they are friendly, aggressive, or indifferent, all beings want only happiness.

Open heartfelt joy arises when we give happiness to others. While the words in the text may sometimes seem to suggest a kind of debasement, it is not about that. A classic image is one where we have two pieces of cake. One piece is big and the other is small, and we don't regard it as a sacrifice to give the big piece to someone we love. If we think in terms of self-sacrifice, then giving becomes heavy and we end up with a sense of "Oh, poor me, I am always giving and giving and everybody else is taking and taking." We end up feeling inwardly deprived and dry. But this practice is actually the opposite of that attitude. The opposite of self-sacrifice is not a matter of promoting our own ego. Rather it is a matter related to giving to others with joy and genuine delight in their happiness.

In Buddhism pride is regarded as being threefold. One aspect involves arrogantly thinking that we are better than others. We may be proud of our looks, wealth, talents, family, or race and feel that we are somehow superior to others. But there is also the pride that comes with thinking we are just as good as others. Then there is the pride that comes with thinking we are inferior to others. All these aspects of pride are self-referential. Some people who are psychologically disturbed feel badly about themselves; they feel inferior and they hate themselves. But still they are absorbed in themselves. They can't think of anything outside of themselves. They want to talk only about their problems, their feelings, and the horrible things that have happened to them. Any talk of others bores them to tears. They want to come back to me through the whole time one is in their company. Pride arises not only from thinking that we are wonderful but also from thinking that we are awful. All these aspects of pride are expressions of the ego.

This sense of pride suggested in the text as a matter of feeling superior, inferior, or equal points to the comparing mind. Whatever comparison we make expresses duality between ourselves and others. As soon as we meet somebody, we normally start to compare. Even when we think, "I am just as good as you are," we have immediately made that separation. An open spacious mind does not compare.

Now of course if we are in a situation where we are always giving out and giving out, it could very well happen that after a while we become like an empty bottle. So we also need to replenish ourselves. In Buddhism, this is usually done through meditation practice, where we fill ourselves up in order to be able to give ourselves out.

Most people think of the nuns of Mother Teresa as going around the streets of Calcutta sweeping up the dead and dying, but what they don't understand is that the nuns pass at least half their day in prayer. They breathe in as well as out, and in this way they can keep going. It strikes me that the sisters of Mother Teresa and her volunteers have trained to see Jesus in everyone they care for—Jesus said that he would come back as the poor and the sick, and so the nuns and volunteers believe that they are not just serving some wretched beggar on the street, but rather that they are serving Jesus. It gives them a tremendous feeling of privilege to be allowed to care for their Lord, and therefore they don't feel the sense of pride that "I am so good to be helping this poor person." They are caring for Jesus, and it is with a sense of honor and of love.

Likewise, in Mahayana Buddhism, it is said that all beings have buddha nature. This means that the essence of our being, the true nature of our mind, is primordial awareness, which is blissful emptiness and clarity. It is beyond time and space and transcends the idea of subject and object. Unborn awareness is likened to the sky. We all have it, not just human beings. Animals, and mosquitoes, too, have buddha nature. Every being that we meet is inherently a buddha. Our tragedy is that we don't realize it and identify ourselves instead with our very ordinary affliction-ridden personality.

We are surrounded by buddhas and bodhisattvas! Isn't that wonderful? If we only saw people as they really are, then we would be overjoyed and honored to serve them. This is not a path for the oppressed—this is a path of joy!

The third verse says:

> In all my actions may I watch my mind,
> And as soon as disturbing emotions arise,
> May I forcefully stop them at once,
> Since they will hurt both me and others.

Now as I am sure you know, dealing with what are called the three or the five poisons is one of the main concerns in Buddhism. Throughout the ages there have been various ways developed to deal with the poisons of ignorance, desire, and anger, together with envy and pride. Until we become an arhat or a buddha, everybody has something of the three poisons, and we all suffer from them to a greater or lesser degree.

This text reveals the conduct of perfectly realized bodhisattvas selflessly giving of themselves, serving others before themselves, completely joyful and fearless in the face of all that they meet. —Well, when considering such matters, we have to be very honest. If we are fortunate enough to really have these qualities, that is wonderful. But it does not help to pretend to ourselves that we are perfect bodhisattvas. If we assume the pose of being perfectly loving and compassionate, without irritation or anger, and entirely filled with loving-kindness toward all other beings, then we create more problems for ourselves than benefit.

It often happens, especially with newcomers to the Dharma or to this kind of doctrine, that when we hear of the actions of bodhisattvas and read about the problems of self-cherishing, we think a genuine practitioner should act like this and never think like that. We force ourselves to become as actors playing a part because we don't want to admit to any negative elements. We suppress our unwholesome emotions, thereby creating what in Jungian psychology is called the shadow. We develop a shadow because we do not face up to the more disreputable parts of our psyche—we believe that we are only allowed to acknowledge the light. Eventually, this causes a crisis. People get nervous disorders and so forth and they become very disillusioned with spiritual practice as they were trying so hard: "I've always tried to be a good person so why is this psychological breakdown happening to me?" And usually, it is because they have not been true to themselves. Even lamas complain about it because people have their ideas of how lamas and gurus and monks should behave. They are expected to act in certain ways—to be ever happy and smiling and however else we imagine a perfect being behaves. We do not allow them to be just who they are. It does not mean that our teachers should be undisciplined and wild, but often they cannot express themselves as a real person. This can feel imprisoning. And if they have any insight into their nature, they know that while they are not bad, they are still human beings. There is a famous line from Shakespeare's *Hamlet,* "This above all: to thine own self be true." When we are true to ourselves, we are naturally honest with others.

The only way to really know what is going on inside ourselves is to look dispassionately. We can lie to ourselves a lot, especially about our intentions and motivations. Usually we give good-sounding motives for whatever we do, and often those motives are not real. We deceive ourselves as to our real intentions in order to feel okay about ourselves. Even Hitler and Mao Tse Tung and Pol Pot felt outraged when anyone questioned whether what they were doing was for the benefit of the masses. They justified everything that they did. As far as they were concerned they were great heroes. We can justify anything, including genocide.

Observing our thoughts without judging them, looking into the quality of our thoughts and feelings, are ways that can really help us to become honest with ourselves. We can just see what comes up. As we progress in our spiritual practice, more and more subtle undertones start to arise. We may see that certain qualities which we had considered acceptable are not okay. Or we may find, delving beneath the surface, that certain qualities that had once seemed suspect are actually fine. According to Buddhist psychology, any action of body, speech, or mind in which the basic intention is tainted by any poison is negative and will result in unwholesome karma. It doesn't matter how we justify these actions to ourselves. If our real underlying motivation is based on our ignorance or desire or anger, on our aversion or jealousy or pride, the results will always be harmful. But if we become aware—if we know what is actually happening in our minds—then we are able to recognize these positive and negative tendencies at the moment of their arising. Often, however, by the time we are conscious of feeling angry or greedy or jealous, we have already been swept along by it. So the sooner we can distinguish what is arising in our minds, the easier it is to just accept it and let go. None of these negative qualities are arbitrary; they are very basic qualities which are interconnected, and their existence derives from this sense of self, this sense of a self-existing autonomous ego, which is our basic ignorance.

It is obvious that once we have this sense of a separate, autonomous ego, the desire to gratify the ego will follow. A desiring, greedy mind reaches out toward anything that appears to be pleasurable—people, things, experiences, thoughts. But sometimes our desires are thwarted and we are unable to get what we want. Or things appear to us to be threatening and painful, and that creates aversion or anger or irritation, as our desire for pleasure has been frustrated. Dukkha, or dissatisfaction, comes, the Buddha said, when we don't get what we want or get what we don't want. The sharper the insight into what is actually going on in the mind, the more we realize that everything we do is polarized between attracting pleasure and avoiding pain. Even when we change our physical position we are inviting comfort and trying to avoid pain. We are as conditioned as a plant that turns toward sunlight and shrinks from the cold, and we do it all the time. Usually we are unconscious of it.

We all have kleshas, afflictive emotions. That is not the problem. But we would do well to become ever more conscious of these negative forces in our mind. We can recognize them and see them for what they are. It is as if we are unmasking a wrong-doer. They shrivel of themselves. Often we don't even need to actually do anything. For example, if we feel irritation arising, we can say to ourselves, "anger." And once we have recognized the anger, of itself it will begin to dissipate. It is not that we have to face anger with more anger—we do not feel angry at ourselves for being angry. That just creates a cycle. When we can recognize that a big angry demon is but a figment of our imagination, it simply evaporates.

These poisons create our problems in life. They are not our friends. On this point, Buddhist texts are very strict. Sometimes the poisons appear innocuous, especially greed, because when our greed is fulfilled it does not feel like a problem. Held in our heart, these emotional defilements are our enemy. They are endless and endlessly agitating. They can never be satisfied. Angry people sometimes feel very self-righteous; anger often feels very justified, so it seems all right. But in fact, to be angry is like having an enemy sitting in our heart. After all, we can try to reconcile with our enemies. We can sign a treaty and even become friends. But when we recognize our enemies the poisons, we can call on the Dharma to help us on the spiritual path. For example, the antidote to greed is contentment, sharing, and generosity. The antidote to anger is patience in difficult situations as well as compassion and love. The antidote to envy is joy and happiness in the other's good fortune; and the antidote to pride, of course, is explained in this text, the *Eight Verses of Mind Training*—to place others before ourselves.

Dharma is to be practiced day by day. It is not reserved just for the meditation hall. It is to be cultivated from moment to moment. And so the fourth verse says:

> When I see ill-natured people,
> Overwhelmed by wrong deeds and pain,
> May I cherish them as something rare,
> As though I had found a treasure-trove.

This verse opens us to the question of what we do when we meet people who are difficult or ill-natured. Normally our reaction is to avoid them or to become irritated or even angry. But in order to genuinely advance on the spiritual path, we need to cultivate compassion and loving-kindness and develop the patient acceptance of difficulties and obstacles. Now if one is a reasonably nice person, usually other people will be pleasant to us in return. That's very good. But it is very easy to be friendly and loving with people who are themselves friendly and loving. Effort is not particularly required. After all, even wolves and tigers are friendly and loving toward their own. But it is no good to exercise by lifting a feather. If we want to develop real spiritual muscles and become a bodhisattva—a spiritual warrior, as it is translated from the Tibetan—we need obstacles to overcome. We need heavy weights. And that is what this text is about—the gratitude we feel toward difficulties and obstacles. This is how we learn. Of course we don't need to invite these difficulties, but when they do come, we know the method to deal with them skillfully.

Atisha, the founding father of lojong, brought an attendant with him to Tibet who was a Bengali monk. This attendant was rude and obnoxious and would never do anything anyone asked of him. Perplexed, Atisha's disciples said, "Look, why do you keep this awful person to attend you? We would really serve you with so much devotion. Please send him back and we will look after you."

Atisha replied, "What are you talking about? He is my greatest spiritual friend. Without him how am I going to put all these Dharma principles into action? You are all so devoted and loving, you are of no use!"

And so this is why the text says of ill-natured people, "May I cherish them as something rare." It is a very skillful way of dealing with people and situations we find difficult. Becoming upset, creating more anger and aversion, only causes more suffering for ourselves. Actually, our anger does not hurt others. They may feel settled in their smug complacency. They are fine. But we are the one who suffers. We are doing for ourselves what only our enemies would want for us. Why give them that satisfaction? And this is the point—depending on our attitude, situations are helpful or not. It is not what is happening out there. It is how we deal with it.

During the Second World War, there was a young Jewish woman in Holland named Etty Hillesum who was in her late twenties. She was an artist and writer leading a fairly bohemian life. She was not really religious; she was just an ordinary sort of person. At that time under the Nazi regime the Jewish people had to wear a yellow Star of David so that everyone would know that they were Jewish. As they could no longer travel on public transport, they could not work. As they were not issued with ration cards, they could not buy most foodstuffs. They were destitute and starving. During the day they were constantly harrassed by Nazi soldiers who were very aggressive, full of hatred, and totally powerful. Then came the routine of arrests in their homes at night so they could be sent to the death camps. It was a time of immense hardship, terror, and fear, and Etty saw all of it. She wrote many letters, and this is how we know of her. Etty later died in one of the camps. In her letters she had observed what was going on around her and wondered, "What can we do? What is the answer to all this hatred and fear and violence?" She wrestled with this and realized that the moment she gave in to hatred and fear, they won. The only answer was love. When she answered their hatred with love, she was victorious.

The *Eight Verses of Mind Training* unfolds for us now in the fifth verse this question of reactivity and defensiveness. Normally when someone criticizes us, we jump in to defend ourselves to prove them wrong. And so the verse says:

> When someone out of envy does me wrong
> By insulting me and the like,
> May I accept defeat
> And offer the victory to them.

We are not trying to be masochistic, but unless it is something really important, what does it matter? We are always willing to take credit when people say good things about us, but why not be equally pleased if people say bad things? If it makes people happy to spread bad things about us, that is their problem.

Actually, praise and blame are just words. If somebody praises us then we should look and see if their praise is valid or not. If it is true, then that is nice. But if it isn't, then they are praising their own projection. Likewise, if someone blames and insults us, we should see if what they are saying is true. If it is true, then the people who criticize us are actually helping us by pointing out faults which we ourselves may not be conscious of. So we should feel grateful. And if it is not true, then what's the problem? The only time when it would be considered acceptable to defend ourselves is if the defamation or insult created some real problems, especially for other people involved. For example, if we are working as a part of an organization and someone spreads untrue rumors about it, creating some obstacles or harm, then it would be fair to set the record straight.

We don't usually hurry to correct others when we are unfairly praised beyond what is actually true. But we are fast on our guard against any criticism! Let's be happy even when others speak badly about us through the force of their jealousy or envy. Let's just relax.

The sixth verse points to the wonderful opportunities we may meet in life to further develop our compassion and patience:

> Even if someone whom I have helped
> And in whom I have placed my hopes
> Does great wrong by harming me,
> May I see them as an excellent spiritual friend.

When we feel let down by those in whom we have placed our trust, instead of feeling upset and betrayed, we can learn to see through it. This is the ultimate test. It often happens in families and other sorts of relationships that those who at one time were close and loving end up as bitter enemies. This is tragic because everybody suffers. Nobody gains. But one could take conflict and transform it. One could see it as a supreme spiritual challenge. Instead of falling into enmity, anger, and bitterness, one could open the heart to understanding and compassion and give love in place of hatred.

But seeing this clearly is hard for human beings all over the world. Parents turn against their children; children turn against their parents; siblings blame each other; husbands and wives divorce with acrimony; business partners fall out. Nobody wins in these situations. This verse offers us a way to turn such situations right around. Instead of ending up angry and bitter for the rest of our lives, our hearts have the remarkable opportunity to open up. The whole point is that we have to use our lives for something worthwhile. If we just carry on with the same kind of reactivity as an animal possesses, then we have basically wasted this lifetime.

The seventh verse refers to a practice which in Tibetan is called *tonglen*. It is traditionally a very popular practice, and most practitioners, great lamas included, engage in it. Tonglen is the practice in which we take the pain and suffering of others and give out our goodness and happiness.

> In brief, directly or indirectly,
> May I give all help and joy to my mothers,
> And may I take all their harm and pain
> Secretly upon myself.

In this practice of tonglen, *tong* means to give out and *len* means to receive: it is a practice of giving and taking. There are two main applications for tonglen: as a meditation practiced for those who are sick or in trouble, and as a meditation practiced for oneself when one is sick and in trouble. But the basic idea is the same in both. The common sense idea would be that we expel all negativities from ourselves and draw in the light. Everybody can understand that. But in tonglen that is reversed. We call in the darkness, and we send out the light. The easiest way to explain tonglen is to simply share in the practice.

Tonglen

Imagine before you someone that you care for, someone who is suffering, either physically or mentally. If you are not good at visualizing, at least get a feeling that this person is with you, right here. Right now. You can even look at a photograph if you have one. The point is to have a sense of their presence and to picture their suffering.

Now, with the in-breath, inhale that suffering in the form of black light or smoke. It is like being a vacuum cleaner: we suck in all this person's pain and all the negative karma that has created it.

Take in this dark light along with the breath. The dark light goes down into the center of our chest, where there is a small black spot, like a black pearl, which represents that deep dark point of our self-cherishing mind. Normally, however much suffering we see in others, and however much compassion and empathy we may feel for them, we still keep something at the back of our mind that says, "I'm glad it's not me!" Drawing in this dark light strikes at that point. It counteracts all our usual instincts for self-preservation.

As the dark light dissolves into the black pearl of our self-cherishing, the black spot instantly transforms into a brilliant diamond that represents the true nature of the mind: luminous, clear, cognizant, pure awareness. And empty! This is our buddha nature, which is always present. Like a diamond, it can never, ever be tainted, no matter how much dirt and darkness is absorbed.

It is important that the incoming dark light strike this small black spot of self-cherishing at the center of our chest. We don't hold our breath; rather, the spot instantly transforms into a diamond of clear pure light that then radiates out on the exhalation.

Just as a diamond cannot ever be defiled however much dirt or mud we stick on it, likewise the pure nature of the mind can never be defiled no matter how much darkness we inhale. The nature of the mind is always totally pure.

So then, from this perfect diamond in the center of the heart radiates out a tremendously bright clear light which represents all our wisdom, compassion, good karma—everything that is positive and good within ourselves. It travels out with the outgoing breath, washes over, and dissolves into the person we have imagined in front of us.

This process of giving and taking rides on the breath. The incoming breath brings in the darkness; the outgoing breath gives out the light. It is a very simple concept.

Tonglen can be very useful when we visit someone in the hospital, or anyone who is troubled or sick or dying. We can just sit there, breathing, engaging in this visualization on their behalf while they are unaware of it. Often when we are in the presence of great suffering we feel so helpless, and this practice is something we can do quietly, without any notice or cause for concern. If we were to get down on our knees and pray or wave incense over our sick friend or relative, it might be embarrassing for all concerned. But with tonglen practice, no one has to know that we are doing the most that we possibly can to benefit them. As to the matter of distance, if our motivation is sincere, then it makes no difference. If we are really concentrating on that person, our ideas of near and far are relative. When we conceive with sincerity that they are present, then tonglen works just the same.

In the Tibetan tradition, tonglen is frequently practiced when one is sick or troubled. When asked what meditations they practice when they are ill or even dying, many practitioners, including great lamas, reply that they practice tonglen. For example, imagine we have cancer. We draw in on our in-breath all the cancer in the world in the form of dark light, and on the out-breath we send out, in the form of light, all the health and happiness from our inexhaustible pure nature and all the good karma we have ever created to all those beings who are suffering from this disease. With tonglen, we make use of what is actually happening. Instead of just lying there, feeling sorry for ourselves, we can use our own difficulties as a means of genuine benefit— for others, through compassion and pure intention, and for ourselves, as we reduce our self-cherishing attitude.

The last verse of our text draws us yet deeper into our self-inquiry.

> May none of this ever be sullied
> By thoughts of the eight worldly concerns.
> May I see all things as illusions
> And, without attachment, gain freedom from bondage.

"May none of this"—meaning all of the verses which exhort us to deepen our understanding and practice of mind training—"ever be sullied / By thoughts of the eight worldly concerns." The eight worldly concerns are gain and loss, praise and blame, good reputation and bad reputation, and pleasure and pain. Usually we all want gain and praise, a good reputation, and pleasure; and usually we try to avoid the other side of these mind states. We should not be motivated, the eighth verse enjoins us, to put others before ourselves just to gain some benefit. As we know, we have to ascertain our strengths and weaknesses and be very honest with ourselves.

There are three levels of involvement as we engage our Buddhist practice. First, we hear or read about the subject. Then, we intellectually absorb it and inquire into it, as we try to understand exactly what it is all about. Finally, we put our learning into action—we try to become what we have intellectually understood. This is very important. It is naive at best to imagine that the minute we try something we become instantly proficient. We need to train in our practice, as with any other skill.

The *Eight Verses of Mind Training* counters all our normal instincts of self-preservation. And so we need not only to hear about it, we need to get used to the idea. Our present-day culture promotes the notion of self and self-enhancement, and how one can manipulate others to gain advantage—or maybe I should say, how to manipulate ourselves for the advantage of others! Naturally then, some of these ideas need time to percolate through our consciousness, and it is not surprising if initially there is resistance. Actually, resistance can be a good sign, because it means that one has understood what these verses imply. If we just think, "Oh, very nice," and put the text aside, this means we have not really understood what is being offered here. Of course all genuine Buddhist practice is about seeing through the delusions of ego and cultivating the path of wisdom and compassion. The *Eight Verses of Mind Training* is a direct confrontation with our self-cherishing mind from the point of view of everyday life, not only our meditation practice on the cushion. And so for that reason, the author of these verses, Geshe Langri Thangpa, enjoins us to be careful of our motivation and not try to practice this bodhisattva path in order to gain a good reputation, for example, so that everybody will exclaim what a lovely and compassionate person we are. The other side of this state is fear: if we do not act like a bodhisattva, we fear people will criticize us and our reputation will diminish. Either way, an impure worldly mentality is revealed. Our motivation should be inspired purely by our deep empathy and compassion for others and our wish to relieve them of their suffering. But may I emphasize here that the Buddha called Dharma the path of joy, and we should not use this teaching of putting others before ourselves as a way to suppress and demean ourselves, or to feel guilty any time we experience delight. That is still an ego-based approach.

A story comes to me. My grandmother was one of those women who, if you took her out and offered to buy her a nice piece of cake, she would say, "Oh no, don't bother. I don't need to have anything special. I am quite happy to just have that little piece over there which doesn't look very good. It's all right. Don't worry about me." Of course you would give her an extra big piece of cake just to make her feel better, but that kind of false self-denigration is not what we are talking about at all.

A clear example of what we do mean is someone like His Holiness the Dalai Lama: when you see him in action, you see that he is always there for others. When they meet him, people are always struck how, in that moment, they are the only one who exists for him. It doesn't matter who they are—he is completely on their side. There was a lovely photo of him that appeared on the cover of a Dharma magazine, and it showed a security guard standing with his rifle. Walking past him, his back to us, His Holiness has put out his hand, touching the man as he goes by. His Holiness is reaching out to him, acknowledging him. And the man is beaming.

His Holiness is always so cheerful. But if you tell him something sad, he will cry—his heart is completely open. He doesn't care about it being considered unmanly to cry. If it is something sad, he just weeps, being completely with you. But five minutes later, he is laughing. There is so much joy emanating from him, and this is the point. His Holiness has such joy because he is not concerned with himself. He is totally concerned with others and with making others happy. And that gives him tremendous energy and delight. It does not make him grumpy or bitter.

At the age of twenty-five, His Holiness attained the Geshe Lharampa degree, which is the highest degree in Tibetan scholastic circles. He is extremely intelligent and learned. He has also engaged in a lot of advanced meditation practices, yet when we meet him he seems so simple. He is not considering, "I am a great pandit; I am a great scholar!" In fact, he always says, "I am just a simple monk." Even hard-core journalists when they meet him are very affected by his presence and often leave their meetings with tears in their eyes. They can't fathom how he has such ability to touch people. But of course, this is true not just of His Holiness the Dalai Lama but of many great lamas. However, since he is the Dalai Lama, we all know him. He is generally the one Buddhist whom the ordinary person the world over knows. And it is very fortunate for us that His Holiness is the image of a Buddhist that most people know. His Holiness recites this very text, the *Eight Verses of Mind Training*, every day. He has based his life on it.

We have been exploring thus far what is called relative bodhichitta. It assumes that there is a subject and an object, and is based on the concept of self and others: one puts others in place of oneself. But this implies duality.

When people are ill-natured, for example, we take them nonetheless to be our spiritual friends. This is all very good, but it assumes that there are self-existent individuals who interact with one another. The last two lines of the eighth verse, however, point us toward ultimate bodhichitta.

> May I see all things as illusions
> And, without attachment, gain freedom from bondage.

Let us consider what are called the three spheres or focal points. This is the understanding that subject, object, and interaction are all non–self-existent. They are empty. For example, if we offer someone a gift, this is good if our motivation is that we want to make her happy. On a relative level, this is meritorious and will create good karma. And if we like this gift a lot, and really want it for ourselves, then giving it away helps to reduce the ego— provided we don't become proud because we are being so selfless! Nonetheless, we are still conceptually bound in three ways. We are bound because we think it is we who are giving; we are bound because we think we have an object we are giving it to; and we are bound because we think we are giving it. Our belief is that all this is actually existent and happening. The view that I as a self-identified *subject* am *giving* to a self-identified *object* actually binds us to samsara, even though the action may be creating good seeds. It is not going to liberate us. But a conceptual understanding, an intellectual understanding of the idea that ultimately there is no one to give, no one to receive, and no actual action can begin to cut away at the heavy causes that bind us to our samsaric mind. Cut away, that is, until genuine realization dawns.

It is very important to have at the back of our mind that even our good actions are non-inherently existent because otherwise even our good actions can be causes that bind us to samsara. This idea of the three spheres of purity also extends to our dedication of merit prayers for the happiness of all beings. And especially, if we offer a donation to someone in need or to our Dharma teacher or center, we can say, "I offer this on behalf of so and so," or, "I offer this for the happiness of all beings," with the understanding that nonetheless, ultimately, there is no one offering, no one receiving, and nothing being offered. Just keep that in mind.

It is in this light, therefore, that it is said in the Buddhist tradition that the world and ourselves are like a dream, a rainbow, a bubble, a flash of lightning. It is all transient and ungraspable. It may all look substantial, but a rainbow is created by conditions, by rain and sun and by so many causes coming together. There is an appearance of a rainbow, but when we try to find it, we cannot. Likewise, in a dream everything seems so real. If it is a frightening dream, we wake up with our heart pounding. But the dream doesn't have any reality outside our mind. A bubble seems very real, but prick it, and it is just empty air.

And this is how we should view our life. Things are not *actually* a dream, they are not an illusion, they are not a bubble; but they are *like* a dream, an illusion, a bubble. Things are not as they appear to us in our ego-based delusion.

QUESTIONS

Q: What do you mean by duality?

JTP: Here duality means the conception of a self-existing subject and a self-existing object. Normally we possess a conception of an *I* which goes together with the idea that everyone else is non-*I*. This is our ordinary relative conditioned mind. Reality has no understanding of this sense of division between self and others. Natural primordial awareness, the clear light empty nature of the mind, does not recognize duality.

All schools of Buddhism recognize that dukkha is caused by our clinging to an ego; that is the root of the problem. As long as we see ourselves as solid, self-existent, and separate from the rest of creation around us, then we are going to suffer because we are endlessly not getting what we want and getting what we don't want. We are in conflict with all the other little globules of self-existent beings who have their own ideas about what *they* want. So there is always going to be disagreement due to this basic duality.

Q: So when you say, "is like an illusion but isn't an illusion," are you saying that reality is like this primordial clear light?

JTP: The texts stress that the world is *like* an illusion, but they are not saying it is *actually* an illusion, because there are two truths, relative and ultimate. On a relative level, a thing appears to exist as we perceive it. It is only relatively true, but it is nonetheless true on its own level. For instance, an object like this table is just made up of protons and neutrons. If I were a physicist, I could tell you that actually it is all basically just empty energy. But if I threw this table at you, it would hurt. Ultimately it is empty, but on a relative level it appears to be solid. Therefore on a relative level there is some truth to it but ultimately that is an illusion presented by the kind of senses that we happen to possess. The point is that things are not what they seem to be. But it is not enough to just intellectually appreciate that. We must actually have direct realization to know it. Only that can transform us.

Q: If you experience everything as illusion, how do you then identify with others' needs?

JTP: I know what you mean but it doesn't seem to work like that. In fact, the more we realize our empty, illusory nature the more tremendous compassion arises, because we realize how trapped these illusory sentient beings are in their illusory conceptions—how they suffer because they don't see clearly.

Wisdom and compassion are conjoined, and that is why they are regarded as the two wings of a bird: they support each other. As compassion grows, so wisdom and understanding develop. As wisdom sees the situation with increasing clarity, overpowering compassion arises. And yet it is all an empty illusion.

Q: Can you tell us about the importance of strong female practitioners in Tibetan Buddhism?

JTP: As in most religious institutions, Tibetan Buddhism is expressed in a predominantly male voice. The books were written by men, almost all the lineage lamas are male, all the examples handed out to us are male. If they say, "Oh, but there were great female practitioners," and you say, "Well, who?" they reply, "Well, there was Yeshe Tsogyal, back in the eighth century; there was Machik Labdron in the eleventh century; and there was Jomo Manmo in the thirteenth century." Easily, by the time you're finished counting on one hand, you've run out of names, whereas the males are like stars in the sky. In this day and age, that is not good enough. Women also have a voice, which is very distinct, and in order to achieve balance in the Dharma, that voice needs to be heard.

Q: How do you think Tibetan Buddhism has affected the Western mind?

JTP: It's very interesting that Tibetan Buddhism took off so well in the Dharma circles in the West. It says that Tibetan Buddhism has got something to offer. When I first came to Tibetan Buddhism, not only was I dismayed to be caught up in it but also I felt it was just too esoteric, too complicated, too irrelevant, really, for the West to be really interested. But Tibetan Buddhism has two great qualities. It has had very great masters who totally embodied the path, at least until recently. You didn't have to know what they were talking about, you just had to be in their presence. They showed us what it is to be a human being. They showed us our potential. And this blew everybody away. Secondly, Tibetan Buddhism took on board everything which was extant in the Buddhist world up to about the twelfth century. It is a huge Dharma supermarket. In most spiritual traditions, you have this kind of method or that one, and if it suits you, wonderful. But if it doesn't suit you, then sorry, you have to go somewhere else. But Tibetan Buddhism has so much, and at first that can be overwhelming. Where do you start? The richness of its skillful means and detail within its levels and approaches is extraordinary. You never can get to a point where you know it all. Even high lamas ask me about my tradition, because they don't know it. The head of a given tradition may not know the others because there is so much.

Tibetan Buddhism contains skillful means to deal with all kind of personalities and needs. Some people are devotional; others are intellectual. Some people like pure meditation; others like things to be very complicated. And there are those who like things to be very simple. It's all there. In Tibetan Buddhism there are many different methods of tummo, inner-heat meditation, from the very simple to the unbelievably complicated, and with all stages in between. They all work. So the commentaries advise that we find one that suits us and stay with that. This applies to all the practices: we can perform extremely complex visualizations or we can maintain a very simple practice. It is all valid. There are extraordinary depths of psychological understanding within Tibetan Buddhism.

Q: Some people are fearful to be alone. Solitary retreat seems too challenging. But maybe understanding aloneness requires the willingness to just be. Do you feel that your experience of solitary retreat through the guidance of your teacher opened you to heartfull contact with others?

JTP: Most people have a problem with being alone because they're not friends with themselves. Of course, ultimately, we are trying to go beyond the ego. We are trying to see through the fabrications of our self-cherishing. But in the meantime, we have to make friends with ourselves and not be our own worst enemy, because the one thing we can never escape from is our own mind. A lot of people when they are alone become very depressed, because they are just hearing very negative recitals of soap operas which the mind is presenting and which they cannot escape from.

People think when you are in solitude or away from others that you are escaping, but actually it is the one time when you can't escape, because there is no outside contact. You can't distract yourself. You have to face whatever comes up in the mind. You can't run away, you can't put on the television or call up your friends. You have to face what is. And so it makes a lot of sense to learn how to accept ourselves instead of being so judgmental and harsh, which just creates a lot of judgment and criticism of others. If we are at home within ourselves, and we have befriended ourselves, then the mind will cooperate and wish to be a good practitioner instead of putting up any opposition. And once we are more at home within ourselves, more at peace, we can begin to question our own assumptions and ideas and memories, and realize how much we fabricate our inside worlds and don't speak truth to ourselves.

We don't know how things really are; we just make up these fantasies continually. Once we start to look at ourselves, to really face ourselves, that also opens up the opportunity to be truly honest and at peace with others. And so then, when we are out with others, we don't feel so judgmental or critical or defensive or paranoid. As we have accepted ourselves, we can accept others, too.

Q: Can you speak a little bit about the *togdenma* lineage and why it's important to resurrect that?

JTP: Our tradition of the Drukpa Kagyu is a practice lineage, and so throughout the ages we haven't had many great scholars but we've had an infinite number of great practitioners. The jewel of Khamtrul Rinpoche's monastery, Khampagar, in Tashi Jong has been its *togdens*, or yogis. While they follow the tradition of Milarepa, they are fully ordained monks. They have dreadlocks and wear white skirts. When they were in Tibet, the Khampagar togdens lived in caves above the monastery. The Sixteenth Karmapa said to me that even in Tibet togdens like this were very rare, and the togdens of Khampagar were highly esteemed. In Tibet, there were also females of this lineage, but after the invasion, none of them seems to have ever gotten out. Many years ago, the Eighth Khamtrul Rinpoche spoke to me of this as he put around my neck a white silk *kata* or scarf, which in those days was rarely received. "In Tibet," he said, "we had so many togdenma. But now this lineage has been broken, and I will always pray that you will reinstate this very precious female lineage." And I have always felt that this is my real commitment. One aspect of this underlying commitment to start the nunnery was that it act as a support system for training a whole new generation of young women to become yoginis. Certainly we hope that the ninth Khamtrul Rinpoche Shedrub Nyima and the yogis of Tashi Jong are supportive of this, as they know that this was the wish of the previous Khamtrul Rinpoche. They have said that they will help.

At the moment, we have five young nuns in three-year retreat, and they are being taught by the senior yogi, Togden Achoe. At the moment all the meditation teachers are male, but sometimes the nuns need a different approach. Things come up which they can't discuss with their male teachers. Feminine energies are different, and the nuns are embarrassed to explain to a man what they are experiencing, which would not be the case if they were explaining themselves to another woman. And women need to have examples. But unless these girls and young women are properly trained, they will never be able to reach that level of stable realization, which requires great guidance and training and many years of dedication.

So this is what we are trying to do. Bringing forth a small group of very dedicated and realized young women is our gift to the lineage and to the world.

Q: For those who are unfamiliar with the divine feminine, how would you describe the power of Tara? And what is your personal experience with Tara?

JTP: It's very interesting that the idea of the divine feminine has always been present everywhere in the world, and despite the insistence through the last millennium or so on a male-only divinity, somehow the feminine has always managed to speak up. Whether we think in terms of Tara or Guanyin or Isis or the Virgin Mary, there is this sense of *mother*. With our father, we may feel that we have to be good and work hard to get his approval; we try to reach up to him. But with our mother, even if we're the naughtiest, ugliest little baby in the world, we are loved; she reaches down to us just as we reach for her. We don't have to keep trying, because for our mother we are the most precious being. She doesn't care who or what we are. She simply loves us. And this quality is very much embodied in Tara. There are many stories of Tara. Sometimes they tell of rascals and of how she has helped them. You don't have to be super-good in order to be helped because she is the mother—she's there to clear away obstacles and to open up opportunities for us to lead our lives properly. Tara is always immediate.

There are many accounts by people who have never met with Tibetan Buddhism who nonetheless have had visions of a green lady wearing beautiful jewels. Sometimes, these practitioners were Catholics who thought they were seeing the Virgin Mary, though afterwards, they thought, "Now wait a minute, she was *green*." One lama, a great devotee of Tara, was teaching when one student said, "I'm willing to do all of these Tara practices"—of course it was a Western student—"and I'll do whatever you say, but I have one question for you. Is Tara real? Is she true? Does she exist?" And the lama thought about it and said, "She knows she is not real."

And that's it. That is the difference between Tara and us—we think we are real.

⤸ 8
Faith and Devotion

B EING BY NATURE very skeptical, I'm not sure if I'm the right person to speak of faith and devotion. But let's do our best to inquire.

The Lord Buddha himself actually put faith at the forefront of the five powers needed in order to attain buddhahood. He described faith as a leaping forward. And in this light he used the analogy of a river without any bridge across it. People who were on one side of this river wanted to proceed to the other side, but they held back. "No, the river is too wide," they said. "It's too deep; it's flowing too fast—we can't make it." They hesitated. But one man who had more courage said, "We can do it. I believe that it's possible to cross." He then crossed the river with that sense of determination and faith. And because he got across, others were encouraged to cross, too. In other words, faith is an expression of confidence. Faith is not a kind of blindness, or a belief in something just because one is credulous.

In Buddhism, faith is an inner confidence in something that is worthy of our trust. For example, we have faith in the Dharma, but that doesn't mean we have to blindly swallow everything we read. Just because it is written in the holy books or because a lama says it, doesn't mean we have to believe it. In the Buddhadharma, that kind of credulous, unquestioning, naive belief is not necessarily considered to be a virtue at all. The quality of questioning in an intelligent manner, really investigating and seeing for ourselves whether something is worthy of our belief or not, is very much encouraged.

And it's not only the Dharma that we are encouraged to question but also the whole attitude about teachers. Sometimes I would go to my lama, Khamtrul Rinpoche, and show him a passage I just could not swallow. He would laugh and say, "Oh, come on! You don't have to believe everything that's written in the books or said in the sutras—it may not be true." At one time he said that a lot of what was written in the books and in the sutras was a result of the particular cultural accretions and superstitions of that time. It's not eternal truth. It's just what they happened to believe at that time, and the Buddha couldn't be bothered to negate it because it wasn't very important. For example, some Westerners grapple desperately with the whole description of Mount Sumeru and the four continents in order to keep complete and unquestioning faith in their lama's teachings.

Once I gave a talk to our youngest monks about the sun and the earth and the moon. I held an apple in one hand and an orange in the other in order to explain that the moon goes around the earth and both go around the sun, and so forth. There was an old monk at the back of the room who said, "Where is Mount Sumeru and the four continents? The earth is flat on the back of a turtle." I said, "Well, as far as we can tell, there is no Mount Sumeru and the four continents. The earth is not flat, it's round." The old monk just nodded and said something like, "Oh well." Maybe in medieval Europe I would have been burnt at the stake for less. But in the world of delusory appearances, flat or round—who cares? We don't have to swallow everything we're told. Being credulous is actually not a virtue. We have to bring our intelligence to everything.

In the Buddhadharma, there are three aspects. First, we hear or study the Dharma. We hear about it, we read about it, and then we think about it. We really think about what we've read or heard; we turn it over in our mind. And if there are any doubts, we ask about them. When our doubts are settled, we go away to contemplate the matter until we become that teaching. We don't just bite off the Dharma and gobble it down in a big lump which then sits like a heavy ball in our stomach. We really have to chew it well until we can swallow it and become nourished by it.

One of the beautiful things about the Buddhadharma is its essential truth. As soon as we hear it, we think, "Oh yes, right!" We recognize the truth of issues like impermanence, the unsatisfactory nature of general existence, the fact that our clinging to an ego gives rise to our problems in the first place. The fact is that these negative qualities of mind like our delusion, our greed and clinging, our aggression and anger, our pride and jealousy and envy afflict the mind and create great pain. This isn't a belief. This isn't a matter of faith. This is a matter of just looking at the situation and thinking, "Yes, that's right!" Whenever our mind is unhappy, if we really look into it, the problem is always these very poisonous emotions in our mind. Our depression is mostly caused by the aggression in the mind. Even if that aggression is turned toward ourselves as it very often is, it's usually based on this root of hatred.

When one looks into the fundamentals of the Buddhadharma, there's something inside us which quickly realizes, "Yes, that's how it is." A sense of confidence may unfold because we think, "If these very basic teachings are so clear and so true, then maybe there are more advanced teachings which my deluded mind cannot yet completely comprehend at the moment." And then if we don't understand something, instead of saying, "No, this is all wrong because I don't understand it and it doesn't agree with my preconceptions," we can say, "Right now I don't understand this. This doesn't accord with how I see things. For now, I'll put it to one side and later, when I have studied and practiced and experienced more, I'll go back and look at it again."

So we're not heretics if we don't have blind faith and a belief in dogmas. It's not like that. Every step of the way, we have to know where we are putting our foot down. We have to understand what it means. We have to question. We have to really investigate and use our intelligence.

In the traditional form of studying philosophy in Tibet, every part of a given text is debated. You must have seen those pictures of people standing up and engaging in these very ritualized debates. They take each section and dissect it while questioning the opponent, trying to trip them up. They each have to defend their position with quotations from the sutras and from the masters of the Buddhist tradition, and not only that. They must engage one another through logic and clear exposition of a given point. In other words, we really have to understand what we believe and what we don't believe, and why we believe it or not. This is very important. We should really inquire into the truth of everything we read. And we should really inquire into the truth of our lives as well.

We can look for and see examples of this. If we don't believe in something, then why don't we believe it? We can go and discuss it with someone who is more learned and more realized than ourselves, and see if they can explain it to us clearly. If they can't resolve the matter for us, then we put it aside for now. And then, from time to time, we bring it back out for our deeper scrutiny, and maybe we say, "Well, it makes more sense now. Why wasn't it clear before?" In that light, in Buddhism, faith is not a blind faith. That's not encouraged. What is encouraged is the kind of confidence that stems from knowing that enlightened masters really are enlightened, really do understand the nature of reality, and can make the whole thing very clear for us.

And what we have to do is trust that when we study, analyze, and look, it will all become very clear.

As we practice and integrate the Dharma into our everyday life, again and again, we find ourselves suddenly saying, "Yes, right, that's what he meant when he said that." The whole thing suddenly comes alive and becomes real. It comes from the head down into the heart and is confirmed. "Right. That's what she meant. Yes."

Devotion is much more tricky. As I go around the world, both in the West and in the East, one of the main questions asked is, "How do I find the perfect master?" I have a friend in Italy who's convinced that somewhere there is the perfect master waiting for him and at a certain point, he's somehow going to meet him. And this master is going to say the word or just gaze into his eyes and say, "You are the one," or something like that, and then this man is going to be enlightened! And if he can't immediately give him enlightenment, obviously he's not a perfect master. Therefore, my Italian friend does nothing. He doesn't practice. He feels that to practice and try to make any effort on one's own side is counterproductive! We just wait until the karma is right and the master appears, and that's it. Even though that's an extreme case, you'd be surprised how many people secretly believe this.

Many people have this fantasy of somehow coming across some yogi or lama sitting on a mountain-top who looks up and says, "Ah, I've been waiting for you. What took you so long?" People think that if they could only find the perfect master who's just right for them, all their problems would be solved. Sometimes I say to people, "Look, even if you meet your master, that's when your problems begin!" In fact, even if the Buddha himself was sitting in front of us right now, what could he do to our untamed and uncontrolled minds?

Tibetan Buddhism emphasizes the lama a lot. There is particular emphasis on what is called the *tsawai lama* or root guru. It should be understood, first of all, that the teachers or lamas from whom we receive ordinations, initiations, teachings, or have any contact with, are not by any means necessarily our root guru.

There are many levels of teachers. There are teachers who bestow the precepts on us. Those are our preceptors. There are lamas who grant us initiations, and those are our initiatory masters. There are lamas who teach us philosophy and the intellectual side of the Dharma, and those are our professors. There are many kinds of lamas. There are lamas we go to for advice and help, and those are our spiritual friends, our *kalyanamitra*. It's actually quite rare to meet with the lama who is our root or heart guru. Traditionally, at least in the Kagyu and Nyingma schools, the root guru is the lama who points out to us the true nature of the mind. The one who points out to us the essential naked awareness behind the conceptual coming and going of the thoughts and who reveals to us our innate buddha nature. That is the root guru.

I was very fortunate in meeting my own lama, Khamtrul Rinpoche, on my twenty-first birthday. Although he passed away in 1980 at the age of forty-eight, he was very quickly reborn and is now in his twenties. He is the spiritual head of the nunnery which we have founded. In all these years he has always been my lama, and he is always still sitting in my heart. In this way, it could be said that I have devotion. And in this I am constant, but that is because Rinpoche for me is what is called a *tserab gyi lama,* which means the lama through all our lifetimes. In each lifetime, when we meet with our teacher again, there is instant recognition from both sides. That is very fortunate because then there's no need to doubt; there's an immediate acceptance. The important thing is that we have to really trust the lama. We have to trust that he understands us better than we understand ourselves. Otherwise, how can he guide us if he doesn't know and see us more clearly than we see ourselves?

It's also possible that we'll meet with teachers with whom we may not have that sense of instant acceptance and recognition, but we like them. We feel a sense of, "This is a good person." Sometimes people meet with lamas and think, "I don't know what he believes, but whatever it is, I'll go for it." There is this sense of instant trust.

But we don't know, and this is where it gets tricky. In our culture, we are very much drawn by charisma. It is a culture of worshiping film stars and rock stars and sportsmen. Even our presidents sometimes end up being the ones who have the most glamour, and we can get very caught up in taking this charisma for genuine inner qualities. Sometimes, the most charismatic teachers are not the ones who have the most genuine inner realization. Some of the most genuinely realized beings are outwardly uncharismatic, totally unassuming, and seemingly ordinary.

His Holiness the Dalai Lama says that according to the tantric texts, we should examine the lama for at least three years and at most twelve years. We should examine him, or as His Holiness puts it, we should "spy" on the lama. Because it's not just how they appear when they are on the throne giving teachings and initiations, but also what they're like behind the scenes. How do they treat their attendants; how do they treat people who are of no particular importance to them? Not how do they treat their big sponsors, but how do they treat ordinary people? Look; watch. Don't be beguiled by the glamour; don't be over-impressed by their reputation; don't be seduced by the fact that they have thousands of students and big organizations. Look; ask around. Ask not just their disciples, but also other people. Investigate, because after taking a lama as our heart guru, we are putting our life on the line to that person. And as they say, if it is not a true guru, then hand-in-hand, teacher and disciple will jump into the chasm.

At a teachers' conference, one very famous Western teacher asked His Holiness the Dalai Lama, "How do we deal with the issue of sitting on a high seat and giving teachings and then how we act in our everyday life as an ordinary person? How do we bridge that gap between the spiritual persona we are giving out to people and who we are behind the scenes?" His Holiness looked blank and said, "What?" So the teacher asked the question in a different way, and His Holiness glanced at the translator again in puzzlement, asking, "What?" The Western teacher tried it again, rephrasing it, and then His Holiness said, "If there is any difference between who you are sitting on your throne, and who you are behind the scenes, then you should not be sitting on that throne." He explained that this does not mean we can't relax, but essentially it has to be one continuity. If we change and become a different person behind the scenes from what we present as the teacher, then we should not be the teacher.

We have to look at our teachers carefully. Are they the same, are they compassionate under all circumstances? That's a very important one. Are they always kind, even to people who are of no importance? Do they get angry? What is their reputation? Are they ethical? If the teacher is male, what is his relationship with his female disciples? Are there male disciples? Are people who have studied with these teachers after many years better people? What are the people around the teacher like? There was a controversial lama who lived in America whom I knew and who was a good friend of my lama, Khamtrul Rinpoche. I asked Khamtrul Rinpoche about him because he was so very notorious. Rinpoche said, "Well, at that level, it's very difficult to know. We have to wait for twenty years and then look at his students. Not two years but twenty years. Give them time to mature, then look."

In the meantime there are, as I said, many levels of teachers. We have

gratitude to every teacher, not just lamas, but to anyone who teaches us anything. Even if they are a little lacking in some aspects, still we remember and
feel gratitude for what we've learned from them. Every teacher we receive
teachings from, every teacher from whom we receive initiations—although
one is very grateful to them, and keeps them in one's refuge tree, they nonetheless don't have to be our heart lama.

Two of his Holiness the Dalai Lama's teachers were the regents of Tibet
during his infancy. They were quite special but on certain levels, they were
failing. One of them had a mistress and children although he was supposed
to be a monk. Now, those regents were trying to kill each other and one
of them succeeded. That is a very heavy thing. And these are some of the
Dalai Lama's teachers. And yet he said, "I know they did these things, but I
still have them in my refuge tree because I remember their kindness to me.
I remember the teachings they gave me, and I remember how they helped
me. But nonetheless I don't close my eyes or condone all the things they did
wrong." Again, there's no blind faith here. If something's wrong, we don't
have to shut our eyes or try to sweep things under the carpet. I keep quoting
His Holiness so that you won't think it's just me saying this!

His Holiness also said that if there are any problems concerning the
teacher, if students have doubts, then they should voice them to the teacher.
There might be, for example, sexual misconduct or any kind of manipula-
tion or doubts about the financial situation. Maybe the teacher is misusing
the offerings to support his family or to support himself. The student should
confront the teacher politely but firmly and say, "Look, why is this happening? I don't understand why you're doing this. Maybe this is not how things
should be done." Then it's up to the teacher. Either the teacher says, "Yes,
I'm sorry, this is a weakness of mine. I apologize. I'll try to get things together
better from now on." Or they say, "Oh no, this is high tantric practice, you
don't understand. This is beyond your level of realization." In which case, His
Holiness says, "you get out." His Holiness also says, although I'm not sure if
I agree with this, "you let everybody know; you don't keep it secret."

Tibetans, like most Asians, tend to sweep things under the carpet and
then replace the carpet as if dirt is no longer there. As if all we have to do
is close our eyes and our mouth for the problems to go away. Perhaps this is
a difficulty with religious organizations everywhere, not just Asia. His Holiness is very unusual in being so outspoken, but he's very concerned that the
reputation of Tibetan Buddhism is in jeopardy because of the conduct of

some lamas. He is also concerned that he himself often doesn't hear about it. People don't like to tell him. Sometimes when he goes to the meditation centers, he is shown smiling with these lamas because he doesn't know they are controversial. Nobody tells him.

I was at a conference where he said, "Look, if you know anything about any lama that isn't right, please tell me. Tell me right now. Or if you don't want to stand up and talk about it, send me a letter. I promise you it will only be kept between me and my secretary, and we'll deal with it, but I have to know." He said this because there are abuses; there are some who whitewash and pretend that it's all part of the tantric practice.

Once I asked my lama, Khamtrul Rinpoche, "Seeing that sexual yoga is the quick path, how come you're all monks?" He replied, "Yes, it's true, it's a special quick way, but you have to be practically a Buddha in order to practice it. It's extremely difficult, extremely precarious, and very few are able to practice it." Another Kagyu lama also said to me that he thought nowadays there was nobody who actually could practice sexual tantra anymore.

I am just telling you this because I think we shouldn't be naive. Faith and devotion do not mean being credulous. We need a lama whom we really connect with, whom we feel is the kind of being who is worthy to inspire us. This being embodies the Dharma in his every action—how he acts, how he speaks, how he thinks. We watch; we look; we see. If there is perfect integrity, then we trust. We connect from the heart, and after that, whatever he does, we accept. That's why we have to be so careful.

Devotion to the guru means that at a certain point we become completely open. The role of the true guru is to show us the nature of our mind. The nature of our mind is our innate buddha nature, which is the same as the guru's mind. You see, we don't go to the guru for his body, or his personality, or even his learning. We go for refuge to his dharmakaya mind and the fact that he embodies dharmakaya—that he himself has realized this and is capable of revealing this to us and guiding us.

The first thing the guru reveals to us is our true nature, our naked awareness behind the coming and going of thoughts, our buddha nature. In order to do that, the guru herself must have realization and the ability to transmit it. The student from his or her side must be open. The connection has been described as a corridor with two doors. The guru opens one door, but the student has to open the other door for there to be space for the wind to blow through. So even though the guru could be the greatest guru in the world, if from our side we are closed, then nothing is transmitted. In order for the student to open, there has to be total trust and devotion. That's why devotion is so stressed.

Devotion can illuminate even a very simple gesture. I knew an older English nun who came to my lama's monastery in Tashi Jong at the time of the annual lama dances. This was during the time of the previous Khamtrul Rinpoche. She was just sitting there watching him dance, and obviously her mind was very open. As he turned, he looked straight at her, and when he did this it was as if her whole conceptual mind fell apart, and she spontaneously realized the nature of the mind. And this, even though he was not her lama, and she'd just gone along to watch the dances! But because at that moment her mind was open, and because obviously she was feeling this very relaxed, open spaciousness while she watched him, he was able to transmit something even while he was dancing.

But that is just the beginning. Once we've seen the nature of our mind, as my lama said, then we can start to meditate. It is not the end, it's the beginning. We need the teacher, the guru, to guide us because each one of us is very unique, coming from a different part of the circle, and each one of us has very different needs. When I was younger, in my lama's community at Tashi Jong, there were three Western nuns. One was from the United States, one was from Holland, and there was myself. We'd often take initiations and oral transmissions together. We would decide on certain practices and ask for the empowerments together with oral transmissions of the text. The lamas would wait and give them to all three of us at the same time. But then the actual teaching on the text we each took separately, even from the same person. We never took teachings together. Each one of us got a slightly different teaching. Just an example, there was one teaching where you had to visualize a mandala of one hundred and twenty different deities: one set outside yourself, one set throughout the body, and one set in the heart. It turned out there are about six hundred different deities we were visualizing, and all of them had three heads and six arms plus a consort, and the colors didn't coordinate. My sisters were told just to visualize it sort of roughly, to just get the feel of it. So when I went to get my teaching, I asked, "Just see it sort of roughly and vaguely?" But the lama said, "No, no, see it very precisely; really visualize each deity very clearly. Then if you can really keep the whole thing in your mind, your mind will very quickly get up very high and become very vast." Each one of us was taught in a very different way with a different emphasis, because we were very different from one another and had different needs. A true teacher understands that.

At first, we all got the same kind of teaching on the same things. We did *ngöndro*; we did certain other practices which everybody does. But after that I would ask Khamtrul Rinpoche, "What shall I do?" And he'd say, "Well, how about such and such a practice?" And I'd reply, "Yes right! Fantastic! Let's do that." Then I'd go back to my Dharma sisters and they would say, "Oh, I hope he doesn't tell us to do that!" So I said, "Well, if that's your reaction, of course he won't." And he didn't. What one person needs is not what another person needs, and the glory of the Tibetan tradition is that there is so much. The true guru will guide you. She will find the practices which you need to make your body and your mind healthy. It is a very person-to-person relationship.

In the meantime, we practice, we practice, and we practice. There are so many wonderful teachers; there are so many books. We are very lucky—we are educated and we can read books. Most Tibetans, even those who are educated, never just sit down and read a book. They wait until someone gives them teachings on a particular book before they read it. If someone goes through it sentence by sentence and explains it, they read it. If we give the average Tibetan, even an educated Tibetan, a book and ask, "Can you explain this?" they'll look at it and say, "Oh no, sorry, I've never been given the teachings on this." And if we insist, "No, no, just these words." They'll say, "No, I can't. I was never taught it."

But we can pick up and read almost any book, because we've been educated to do so. How lucky this is. We can go to many teachers, and many teachers come through and give teachings. How extraordinarily fortunate this is. We can practice. There are practices which everyone can do. But first, we have to clear our mind. It's like we are vessels which are filled to the brim with dirty water. Now, even if the most perfect Buddha came with nectar, how could he pour it into a glass which was already filled with dirty water? First we have to empty out the glass, and we have to clean the glass to make it ready to receive the nectar. Otherwise, whatever is poured in will become contaminated. As long as our minds are full of the poisons of the negative emotions, and the garbage and junk of worn-out opinions and memories and judgments, where is there room?

If you have been to Tibet, you know it is empty. Once you get outside of Lhasa, the emptiness is noticeable. You can go days and days and hardly see a tree or a building and almost never a person. Empty. So when Tibetans prepare their decorations or when they paint their thangkas, look—they leave no space! No space, because outside there is so much space. Likewise, the Tibetans' mind was traditionally quite empty. No television, no magazines, no novels, no movies—nothing, just lots of empty space. And so they fill up that vast space with extremely complex visualizations and extremely complex philosophy, because there is lots of room.

But our Western minds are mostly crammed full, and mostly with garbage. So where can we put those precious seeds of the Dharma? How can we plant them in the garbage bin? We have to prepare the garden of our mind—throw out some of the rubbish, dig in there, pull out the weeds, toss out the stones, and get the land ready. We have to really work at preparing the soil. Then, when someone comes along with the perfect bodhi seeds and plants them, they will grow—provided that we water them, fertilize them, and give them the sunshine of the blessings. Only in this way can we absorb the teachings and use them. Otherwise, not even the greatest teachers can have much effect.

Each one of us has to look into our own mind and see clearly what is there and what needs to be done in order to prepare ourselves to accept and practice and become one with the perfect Dharma. It's a challenge; it's not easy. But the lamas are here. They are very compassionate, and they come again and again to the West. They sow their Dharma seeds everywhere in the hope that some of them will flourish. But to make it worthwhile, we have to prepare the soil. We have to be worthy vessels. No one else can do this for us. Even the most perfect guru can't tread the path for us. Each one of us has to tread it for ourselves.

&ⁿ QUESTIONS

Q: I am sure that as a female monastic you are often asked questions about gender. Do you feel the gender of one's teacher is important?

JTP: Obviously whether one's teacher is male or female plays a role. But the important thing is the sense of trust and commitment to the teacher, whatever gender they happen to be. And I feel also that many of the highest lamas in the Tibetan tradition manage somehow to transcend gender: they are both mother and father. So I don't think we should make a big issue about it. I think that it's more a matter of one's karmic connection with the teacher rather than whether they happen to be male or female.

Q: What do you feel are the most important qualities to look for before taking a teacher? And additionally, how much of the responsibility is on the teacher to check up on the students before taking them on?

JTP: From the student's point of view, of course the most important issue is that of trust. If you are going to take someone as a guide, first of all you have to believe that they know where they're going because they've been there. So that's the first thing—that they embody the personal qualities that we ourselves are striving to acquire. Secondly, one should truly trust that the teacher knows the student better than the student knows herself or himself and therefore really understands what is best for the student. And thirdly, there has to be some kind of inner karmic connection, some sense of recognition that this is the teacher. Because you can meet very, very great teachers, and you think, "Yes, they are wonderful," but you don't feel any particular connection with them. You could meet someone else who is not such a great teacher but nonetheless feel this heart connection. So it's a very personal, individual thing. It's not that there is just one world teacher for everybody.

Q: So it's also good that it takes time, this process of choosing your teacher?

JTP: Well, I would like to say so, but I chose my lama before I even met him, so I can't really act as a good example of that. But normally speaking, one is encouraged to test the lama first, to try to really look, if possible, as the Dalai Lama suggests, to find out what they are like when they are not sitting upon their throne—how they treat ordinary people, how they treat their attendants, how they treat people who are of no particular importance to them. Do they really embody the qualities which they talk about? As much as possible we should try to examine this. And I do think the teacher should also examine the student, because many people come to the Dharma who might be better off first getting some psychological therapy. Their reasons for seeking a teacher are sometimes not really the highest, they are very unstable, and therefore their needs may not really be met in the traditional student/ teacher relationship. It might even aggravate the problem for them. On the whole, teachers are not very discriminating. They are more inclined toward numbers than quality.

Q: If one has taken a teacher and then sees them behaving badly or in seemingly inappropriate ways, what advice do you give students who are interpreting this? Is it even acceptable to leave a teacher once you have made a commitment to him?

JTP: Personally, I think that we should never completely surrender our own integrity. I think that it's a big mistake to think that once you have taken on the teacher that's it, and whatever he does you have to see it with pure perception. Of course, you know, one can point to Naropa and Tilopa and Marpa and Milarepa, but nonetheless I think that's quite dangerous.

The point is that the students are the children and the teacher is the parent. A good parent helps the child to mature properly, to not endlessly be a child. And if a parent is abusive, then just because they are the parent doesn't mean that the child should be left in their care. If a teacher really acts inappropriately or requests inappropriate behavior on the part of the student, then the student has the right, also as a human being, to say, "No, I'm very sorry, I don't accept that," or, "Well, okay, explain why you're doing this." And if the teacher will not explain, or their explanation doesn't ring true, then I think it's perfectly appropriate to say with all due respect, "Well, I'm sorry, I am going to find someone else." Because quite frankly, many teachers, even though they might be very charismatic and even have some genuine experience and realization, might also have a big shadow which they're not facing and which their culture doesn't encourage them to face. And in dealing with that shadow, we have to use our common sense. If the relationship creates a lot of inner distress and trauma, then this is spiritually not in the least bit helpful. So without creating a lot of publicity or difficulty, one can just simply say, "Thank you very much for all your teachings," and leave.

I don't think the Tibetans themselves have really resolved this point. We see the teacher as the Buddha, first of all so that we don't get attached to the personality and the appearance of the teacher. We're not going for refuge to their personality; we're going for refuge to their buddha nature, which they have realized and we have not, and to their ability to transmit that realization. So therefore one sees them in an idealized form. But at the same time, we have to realize that we are doing that for the sake of devotion and they are also human beings. If occasionally they act inappropriately—for example, they lose their temper over something about which there is no reason to lose your temper and they really are angry—then one can say, "Well, they are also human beings and it doesn't matter; they have given so much through teaching and they have so many good qualities," and leave that aside. But if they consistently are acting in questionable ways—like being very greedy, or wanting sexual relationships with their students, or accumulating a lot of money and then giving it to their family or building themselves great palaces and starving their monks, et cetera—then I think it is perfectly valid to question their conduct. Even in the ordinary world people don't act like this.

Q: The teacher/student relationship is fundamental in Tibetan Buddhism. In reality, in the West, only a few can be so lucky to have a traditional guru/ student relationship. So, often it happens to a practitioner that after some years there is less enthusiasm and interest. What can you advise to those in such a situation?

JTP: The important thing is to realize that even in a traditional guru/student relationship, it's not really so necessary to always be around the guru. Once one has made a connection, even if one doesn't see the guru very often and the guru is very far away, still one can keep the inner heart connection. For example, in the Tibetan tradition, there are very beautiful prayers for calling on the guru from afar. And especially if these are set to a melody and one can sing them from the heart, they create that connection with the guru, because it's a mind-to-mind connection. Sometimes, even if the lama is sitting in front of you, you can feel there's a thousand miles between you; likewise, you can be a thousand miles away and feel that the guru is right there, sitting in your heart. It's not distance. That is not the true guru. So therefore, to develop a devotion to the guru, you don't need proximity. At the same time, one has to realize that the ultimate guru is one's own buddha nature: it's the nature of the mind, and one has to cultivate being able to be centered within one's own innate awareness and not depend so much on an external relationship. Because when one is in the nature of the mind, then one is indeed one with the guru. This is why when we do guru yoga we absorb the guru into ourselves—to realize that his or her mind and our own mind have become one. This is very important to realize. The ultimate guru is our own innate wisdom, and if we can access and cultivate that, then the enthusiasm for the Dharma just bubbles up endlessly. It doesn't depend on external shots of inspiration from an actual person.

Q: Perhaps our misunderstanding is that having a guru means that we ought to have one single teacher and very strong devotion to that special person?

JTP: But the lamas themselves often have many gurus. Very few lamas actually just have one. Even Atisha had lots and lots of teachers. His Holiness the Dalai Lama has at least twenty-five main teachers whom he considers his root gurus. If you ask most lamas they say, "Oh yes, there is this one and that one and that one and that one." They're not necessarily just centered on one. Also, if one is open and sees everybody as an expression of the root guru, then teachings come from many sources.

9
Practicing the Good Heart

MANY YEARS AGO, His Holiness the Dalai Lama came to the remote Lahaul Valley in India where I was living. He was there for about one week, giving Dharma talks and empowerments. After one of his talks, which had lasted for several hours, I turned to one of the Lahauli women and asked, "Do you know what he was talking about?"

She said, "I didn't catch much. But I understood that if we have a good heart, that's excellent." And that is basically it, isn't it? But let's explore just what we mean by a good heart.

In the West, we have so many material things. But for many of us there is still a profound sense of lack, an emptiness inside, which we are unable to fill. Though we may strive to fill that void with televisions, cars, or houses, the problem is not one of how much or how little we have. Rather it is a matter of whether we believe material possessions will really bring us deep-seated satisfaction. This is actually an advantage for the West: if we can get over our sense of wonder at material possessions, we can begin to see that there is something beyond them. We have this untold wealth within us, and this is what the spiritual path is all about.

There is a need, an urgency now, that we become spiritually mature. Opening to our human potential, believing in it—we have to stand together and support each other. It is not the time to be paranoid and parochial, fearful and insular; it is not the time to close our borders within and without. Fearfulness expresses immaturity. A genuinely adult person is fearless. As was said earlier, *bodhisattva* means a being who strives for enlightenment out of compassion for the world; in Tibetan, literally a spiritual hero. And we do have to be very courageous to stand up to what is happening around us. We have to support and respect each other's integrity as human beings, and we have to use our lives in a way which is genuinely meaningful. Rather than wander around as spiritual beggars, as we normally do, we have to learn how to come back into the spiritual wealth that is within us.

I remember when I lived in Nepal, every morning on my way to visit a lama I would pass an old beggar woman on the worn steps of Swayambhunath Stupa. She was destitute and skinny. I never saw anybody take care of her, or even come near her, and yet inwardly she seemed very joyful. Smiling, she always greeted me. One morning she looked especially radiant, and I thought, "She is going to die." And in fact, the next day she was gone. We might well ask, what did she have to be so happy about? Why did she have this inner joy bubbling up?

During the Cultural Revolution in Tibet, many lamas were sent to prisons and hard labor camps for ten or twenty years or more. They were continually abused, tortured, and interrogated. And by rights, if they had survived, they would have come out completely traumatized, broken, and bitter. No doubt there were Tibetans who went through this experience and came out traumatized. But one can meet with lamas who went through these terrible experiences, and far from being crushed, they are joyful and welling over with an inner happiness. I met a great master of the Drukpa Kagyu lineage, the late H.E. Adeu Rinpoche, and said, "Your twenty years in prison must have been very difficult."

"Oh, no, no. It was just like a retreat!" he said laughing. "Do you know, they even fed us?"

Another lama said to me, "I am so grateful for that opportunity. I really learned compassion. Before, compassion was a word debated in philosophical schools. But when you're faced with someone who only wants to harm you, then there is this question of whether you fall into resentment and fear, or surmount that and have tremendous love and compassion for your tormentor."

Whatever our external circumstances, in the end happiness or unhappiness depends on the mind. Consider that the one companion whom we stay with, continually, day and night, is our mind. Would you really want to travel with someone who endlessly complains and tells you how useless you are, how hopeless you are; someone who reminds you of all the awful things that you have done? And yet for many of us, this is how we live—with this difficult-to-please, always-pulling-us-around, tireless critic that is our mind.

It entirely overlooks our good points, and is genuinely a very dreary companion. No wonder depression is so prevalent in the West!

We have to befriend and encourage ourselves. We have to remind ourselves of our goodness as well as consider what may need improvement. We have to remember, especially, our essential nature. It is covered over, but wisdom and compassion are ever present. In the West, we so often undercut ourselves because we don't believe in ourselves. The first time I met His Holiness the Sixteenth Karmapa, in Calcutta in 1965, he said to me within the first ten minutes, "Your problem is that you have no confidence. You don't believe in yourself. If you don't believe in yourself, who will believe in you?" And that is true.

Since beginningless time we have been utterly pure and perfect. According to the Buddhist view, our original mind is like the sky. It has no center and no limit. The mind is infinitely vast. It is not composed of "me" and "mine." It is what interconnects us with all beings—it is our true nature. Unfortunately, it has become obscured by clouds, and we identify with these clouds rather than with the deep blue eternal sky. And because we identify with the clouds, we have very limited ideas regarding who we really are. If we truly understood that from the very beginning we have been perfect, but that somehow confusion arose and covered our true nature, then there would be no question of feeling oneself unworthy. The potential for enlightenment is always here, for each one of us, if we could but recognize it.

Once we acknowledge this, then our words about having a good heart can truly make sense. Because then we are expressing our essential nature through kindness, compassion, and understanding. It is not a matter of trying to develop something that we do not already have. Seeing this through the lens of another metaphor, we may feel that opening to our essential nature is as coming back to a pure spring. Inside us, we have a spring of everlasting wisdom and love. It is ever-present and yet it has become blocked, and we feel dry within ourselves, as dry as the earth can be. Clinging to all these terribly false identifications, we do not recognize the pure fathomless spring underneath.

The point is that when our mind is filled with generosity and thoughts of kindness, compassion, and contentment, the mind feels well. When our mind is full of anger, irritation, self-pity, greed, and grasping, the mind feels sick. And if we really inquire into the matter, we can see that we have the choice: we can decide to a large extent what sort of thoughts and feelings will occupy our mind. When negative thoughts come up, we can recognize them, accept them, and let them go. We can choose not to follow them, which would only add more fuel to the fire. And when good thoughts come to mind—thoughts of kindness, caring, generosity, and contentment, and a sense of not holding on so tightly to things any more, we can accept and encourage that, more and more. We can do this. We are the guardian of the precious treasure that is our own mind.

When the Buddha spoke of the practice of loving-kindness, he said there were two ways in which to engage it. We could send out thoughts of love in all directions—north, south, east, west, up and down and everywhere. Directionless, we radiate loving-kindness to all beings in the world. Or, the Buddha said, we could begin our practice with the people we like—our family, partner, children, friends—over time extending our range to people we feel indifferent toward and then to people we dislike. Eventually our practice of loving-kindness reaches out still further to embrace all beings everywhere. But before doing any of this, the Buddha said that we are to begin our practice by radiating loving-kindness to ourselves. We start by thinking, "May I be well and happy. May I be peaceful and at my ease."

If we do not first feel that sense of kindness toward ourselves, how are we ever going to be kind to others? We are opening to love and compassion for all sentient beings—humans, animals, insects, fish, birds—beings both seen and unseen, beings in the higher realms and in the lower realms, beings throughout the universe. All sentient beings are the object of our love and our compassion. So how is it then that we omit the being right here, the one who is opening to this endless love? Practicing like this would be like radiating light while standing in the dark. And that is not right. We must first extend our loving-kindness toward the being who is also in need: oneself. This is very much part of what it means to develop a good heart.

When I was with my own lama, Khamtrul Rinpoche, I would think he was like a mountain. I mean, he was a big man. But he was like a mountain because he was so unshakable, and I would think, "Even if the sky fell down, Rinpoche could deal with it." He gave the impression of being completely capable in all situations; nothing could ruffle him. There was a tremendous sense of quiet power. Another student once said to me, "Why is it that when Rinpoche just drinks a cup of coffee it has so much significance, but when we drink it doesn't mean anything?" And it was true!

Once, in a dream, I was in a theatre in the wings. On the stage was a very high throne, and on it was sitting His Holiness the Sixteenth Karmapa. All the spotlights were shining on him. The audience was there. And before their eyes he was transforming himself into all the various peaceful and wrathful deities. I remember thinking, "Well, that's pretty wonderful, but it's a bit ostentatious." And then I turned, and saw that my lama Khamtrul Rinpoche was also standing in the wings, watching His Holiness. And then as I looked at Khamtrul Rinpoche I saw that inside him were all the deities, while on the outside, he just looked like a lama. He gave me that look which said, "Do understand!" I realized then that it was His Holiness the Karmapa's activity to show all these wonders. But I also realized that it was Khamtrul Rinpoche's activity to keep it all hidden. And both were really the same. Each was manifesting his Buddha activity in a different way. So, some lamas are more forthright. Others are very hidden. But it is the quality of their inner realization that counts.

A genuinely good heart is based on understanding the situation as it really is. It is not a matter of sentimentality. Nor is a good heart just a matter of going around in a kind of euphoria of fake love, denying suffering, and saying that all is bliss and joy. It is not like that. A genuinely good heart is a heart that is open and alight with understanding. It listens to the sorrows of the world. Our society is wrong to think that happiness depends on fulfilling one's own wants and desires. That is why our society is so miserable. We are a society of individuals, all obsessed with trying to obtain our own happiness. We are cut off from our sense of interconnection with others; we are cut off from reality. Because in reality, we are all interconnected.

Let us start from where we are. And let us start with who we are. It's no good wanting to be somebody else; it's no good fantasizing about what it would be like if we were this or that. We have to start from here and now, in the situation that we are in. We have to deal with our family and friends and all whom we meet. That is the challenge. Sometimes we avoid our present circumstances and think that surely we will meet with the perfect situation somewhere. But that will never happen. There will never be an ideal time and place because we take the same mind with us everywhere. The problem isn't out there; the problem is usually within us. And so we need to cultivate our inner transformation. Once we have developed our inner change, we can deal with whatever happens.

The Buddha spoke of the truth of suffering and the cause of suffering. The cause of suffering is grasping. We hold on to things so tightly because we do not know how to hold them lightly. But everything is impermanent. Everything is flowing. Nothing is static or solid. We cannot hold to anything. Holding on causes us so much fear and pain. It is not an expression of love. Love opens the heart. A loving heart expresses, very simply, "May you be well and happy." It does not say, "May you make me well and happy." The term "heaven" implies that in the end, all our problems will be forever resolved. But in the Mahayana ideal, our motivation is to perfect ourselves solely that we may become the servant of others throughout eternity. In this light, we may imagine: If there were no great masters in the world, what would beings do? There would be no hope.

I once had a dream in which I was escaping from a very frightening totalitarian state. Just as I was about to cross the border to a safe and beautiful country, I thought, "How is it that I am able to escape? From my side, I have really done nothing—so what is it that is allowing me to escape like this?" As I looked toward the customs point at the barrier, I saw a man standing there, watching me, and I thought, "It's him! What is he doing here? He doesn't even belong to this horrible country. He belongs to that beautiful, free country. He doesn't have to live here. But if he didn't, people like me could never get out! It's because of him that I am free." I woke up crying and recollected that the man in the dream was my lama, Khamtrul Rinpoche. He was wearing lay clothes, but it was certainly him. I was so overwhelmed by the dream, by the understanding of his incredible kindness and compassion and of what he had to suffer, when he didn't need to at all. He simply suffered out of compassion for beings like me who could not manage without him. That is what a high bodhisattva is. They do not need to be in this world—they could just groove it out in some wonderful Buddha Pure Land, but yet they come back here. Bodhisattvas come back to help us out of pure unconditional compassion. And this is what we open to within ourselves.

The bodhisattva aspiration leads us to enlightenment, to the fullness of wisdom and compassion, so that we may be of eternal benefit to others. It is a most profound aspiration. One aspires to be a bodhisattva not in order to reach out for the bliss of paradise, heaven, or any kind of pure land, but rather to come back, again and again, in whatever form that will be of benefit to others—wherever there is need. Bodhichitta is the generation of great compassion, which is all-encompassing. It extends to all beings everywhere. Such compassion cannot rest for even one moment in idle bliss and pleasure—it is ever-present for the sake of others. Bodhichitta is expressive of the interconnection of all beings. And we are all interconnected.

Our exploration of compassion may seem a bit heavy, but if we look at Chenrezig, the Bodhisattva of Compassion, we can see that he is smiling. All the bodhisattvas are smiling. There are none that are weeping or in anguish. When we meet great lamas and teachers from other traditions, we may note not only their inner tranquility but their radiance! When we are in their presence, we feel peaceful and happy. Although the task of liberating all beings may seem difficult, we learn through our spiritual practice to see the situation as it truly is. As we open to the wisdom and compassion within us, as we open to our inherently empty spacious nature, we find that everything lightens up. Perceiving at a very deep level that it is all just a dream from which we can wake up, we can truly smile.

᥍ Acknowledgments

I EXTEND a deep debt of gratitude to Camille Hykes, who selflessly offered to take up the mountain of my transcripts and tapes—often boringly repetitious—and transform these ramblings into a sequence of coherent chapters. Without Camille this book would not now be in your hands. My appreciation for all the time and effort that she has expended on this formidable task is boundless.

All of the teachings in the book have been recorded and transcribed by dedicated teams of volunteers in many countries. I am so grateful for their willingness to undertake this time-consuming task.

I would like to warmly thank Evan Zazula and Deborah Garrett, co-directors of the DGL Nunnery Endowment Fund. This book would not have happened without their support and encouragement.

My sincerest appreciation goes to Monica Joyce, our Nunnery Project Director, and my assistant Heather Conte, for going through the edited transcripts and making valuable suggestions and amendments.

Finally, my heartfelt thanks to Susan Kyser of Snow Lion Publications, who went through our manuscript with great sensitivity and a skillful eye, suggesting many excellent amendments to polish this text ready for publication.

The Dongyu Gatsal Ling Nunnery Project

DONGYU GATSAL LING NUNNERY was founded in Himachal Pradesh, northwest India, in 1999, at the request of His Eminence Khamtrul Rinpoche, head lama of the Khampagar Monastery, in order to provide an environment where young women from Tibet and the Himalayan border regions could come together to study and practice in accordance with the Drukpa Kagyu tradition of Tibetan Buddhism.

These young women are given the opportunity to develop their intellectual and spiritual potential through a balanced training of study, meditation, and service. At present their program includes philosophical study and debate, ritual, Tibetan language and writing, English language, and hatha yoga. The nuns also gather for daily ceremonies and meditation.

The special aim of the Dongyu Gatsal Ling Nunnery is to re-establish a precious lineage of yogic practice particularly emphasized in the Drukpa Kagyu lineage. Although there are still a few monk exemplars of this yogic tradition presently residing at the Khampagar Monastery, it seems that the female line was annihilated during the Cultural Revolution.

As it is an oral tradition, handed down from master to disciple, it is essential that this rare and precious practice is passed on while there are still living masters. The yogins of Khampagar Monastery have agreed to train the nuns who show the necessary qualities and potential, once they have completed their studies and preliminary meditation practices.

If you would like to help support the Dongyu Gatsal Ling Nunnery, please contact them through the e-mail address given on the website http://www.tenzinpalmo.com, or write to Dongyu Gatsal Ling Nunnery, PO Padhiarkhar, via Taragarh, District Kangra, H.P. 176081 India.

All proceeds from the sale of this book will go to the DGL Nunnery Endowment Fund, which has been set up to help secure the future of the nuns. If you would like more information about this, please email: endowment@gatsal.org.